WHAT MAKES A CHRYSLER RUN?

Iacocca watchers long have recognized that he manages as he motivates, motivates as he manages. In what some have called "the age of the manager," this book endeavors to present a guide to the amazing track record of an undisputed master of the art of managing. His character strength, knowledge, and grasp are awesome in a top corporate executive facing so many disparate decisions.

No one has dominated the automotive scene as he has. The Iacocca connection is the most powerful advantage any auto company ever had. Power and its application, then, are what this book is all about.

THE
IACOCCA
MANAGEMENT
TECHNIQUE

Maynard M. Gordon

BALLANTINE BOOKS • NEW YORK

Library of Congress Catalog Card Number: 85-12988

ISBN 0-345-33482-5

This edition published by arrangement with Dodd, Mead & Company, Inc.

Manufactured in the United States of America

First Ballantine Books Edition: September 1986

To the most wonderful family
any writer could have:
my wife Lucille...
our children Julian,
Elizabeth, and Adam

CONTENTS

PREFACE

"Chrysler's Le Baron. He's hard-charging and ram-rough, but Iacocca is a family model, too."

"A Spunky Tycoon Turned Superstar. Straight-talking Lee Iacocca becomes America's hottest new folk hero."

"Iacocca: America's Wonder Is 'Consumer Enemy No. 1.'"

"Japan-Basher Iacocca top headliner in Tokyo."

"The two Iacoccas. He's often brilliant on the turn-around at Chrysler, often paranoid on his career at Ford."

"The Miracle in Detroit. Lee Iacocca is the man behind the miracle and today's role model for macho men everywhere. He speaks about health, heroes, Italian cooking, Catholicism, family solidarity, the Presidency, and his new AUTObiography."

"Iacocca should keep selling cars and stay out of politics."

"Is there life after Iacocca? Can Chrysler keep it up?"

The above headlines frame the story of one executive's cometlike rise to national stardom as the savior of a moribund auto manufacturer. Lee Iacocca's name has become a household word, with recognition and approbation such that he has been seriously mentioned as a Democratic Presidential candidate in 1988.

What the headlines and the hype omit from their breathless phrases is how Iacocca perceived his management style and then executed his command decisions, first as president of Ford Motor Company and then as chairman of Chrysler Corporation. What enabled Iacocca to achieve the miracle of Chrysler's rebirth—and how did he surmount the innumerable obstacles in his path?

This book endeavors to trace the evolution of the Iacocca style, not as a psychohistory or an adulatory "campaign biography" but in terms that can be useful to admirers and objective students alike. It is not every day that a successful president of a mammoth automotive producer is fired, only to take charge of a dying competitor and bring about its total resurrection. Not since 1940, moreover, when a utilities executive named Wendell Wilkie captured the Republican presidential nomination has a corporate leader been seriously mentioned as a presidential prospect. At sixty-one, as of October 15, 1985, exactly as old as the Chrysler Corporation that he brought back from the cemetery's edge, a new career at the head of his country's government may lie in store for Lee Iacocca.

Whether Iacocca's managerial conduct, or that of any comparable chief executive officer of a large corporation, could work effectively in the White House is a matter of keen debate. American companies, despite ownership by stockholders who elect directors nominally every year, are not democracies. The officers chosen by the directors make the decisions, which are almost never disapproved by those same directors. The chief executive officer, usually the chairman of the board, selects the directors he wishes to "work with" and has absolute authority not dissimilar to that of the Popes in Rome or the Czars in Russia of old.

Rarely has the business world focused so minutely on the whys and wherefores of its high-achieving "supermanagers." The "search for excellence" goes on at a feverish pace. The Iacocca style and story is told in this book in the hope of shedding more light on how he accomplished his career rise at Ford and then performed "mission impossible" by resurrecting a nearly extinct Chrysler and guilding it to record sales and profits in a mere six years.

Iacocca watchers long have recognized that he manages as he motivates, motivates as he manages. In what some have called the "age of the manager," this book endeavors to present a guide to the amazing track record of an undisputed master of the art of managing.

In his autobiography and in some insightful interviews, Iacocca makes it clear that he blended in with the corporate system at Ford and Chrysler as an ambitious aspirant for power and as an unabashed emperor when he reached the top. He does not, however, touch on the errors of omission and commission in his thirty-nine-year career, or on the rollercoaster history of Chrysler Corporation and its strong-willed rulers before he got there.

Yet the story of Iacocca's rise to the status of a "household word" and a *primus inter pares* is far more than a business-school thesis on his style vis-à-vis that of managers of other enterprises. The Iacocca "mystique" of the mid-1980s probably would never have reached such proportions without a mixture of elements: His training up the corporate ladder at Ford, Chrysler's checkered history, the timing which made him available to take charge of a battered Chrysler, a sympathetic administration in Washington, an amazing ability to exploit opportunities on his part and at the same time arouse support from employees, dealers, government leaders and the public.

The measure of the effectiveness of any top business leader is what happens to the enterprise when he leaves. It is his ultimate test to create a viable succession in senior management ranks. The embittered Iacocca leaves little doubt that he expected (or hoped) that Ford Motor Company would fall apart after he was expelled by Henry Ford II in 1978. How has he now provided for Chrysler's future leadership—and will he be too tough an act to follow at the Number Three automaker?

This book covers two eras in automotive history and is the work of a journalist who has been active for forty-one years throughout the post-World War II period, and who has seen auto barons come and go between 1944 and 1985. No "survivor" working today has dominated the automotive scene like Iacocca, to the extent that an executive at the Chrysler corporate ad agency calls the Iacocca connection "the most powerful advantage any auto company ever had."

Power, then, and its application by one of its most competent users in many years are what this book is all about.

1

ROOTS AND
ROLE MODEL

OW DID LIDO ANTHONY IACOCCA, A SELF-starter who became one of the auto industry's most celebrated "people movers" and motivators, make the quantum leap from being the son of Italian immigrant parents to scaling the heights of American management?

Iacocca's father was a stern taskmaster of the old school, to hear Lee recall his childhood in Allentown, Pennsylvania; Nicola (Nick) Iacocca had become a successful real estate operator there after the Depression wiped out an earlier, similar business. Nick's expectation for his son, who was born October 15, 1924, two years after a daughter Delma, was that he would excel at whatever he pursued.

There were no ifs, ands, or buts, as far as Iacocca Senior was concerned.

In Lee's case, the apple did not fall far from the tree. "The kind of people I look for to fill top management spots are the eager beavers," he recently wrote, just as, when younger, he himself always brought home the good grades that Nick expected and was graduated twelfth in a high school class of more than one thousand.

Iacocca's middle name, Anthony, stems from his mother's first name, Antoinette. A native of Naples, Antoinette Iacocca was a superb preparer of Italian cuisine. To this day Iacocca prides himself on sharing in cooking chores (pastas are a favorite) with his younger daughter, Lia, at their Bloomfield Hills home, north of Detroit. He is a hands-on participant in all areas, as technical types who have worked for him at Ford and Chrysler have sometimes all too painfully learned.

A bout with rheumatic fever in the tenth grade affected Iacocca's life in many long-lasting ways. Though his heart was not damaged, he was compelled to give up sports. A 4-F draft deferment status in World War II resulted, giving Iacocca an unconscious "chip" to shoulder later on when he tangled at Ford with the crew of Air Force "whiz kid" officers recruited by Henry Ford II.

As a result, Iacocca channeled his considerable ambition into school studies and oratory. It's safe to say that his development as a skilled communicator began with his childhood illness, although he was left with a near-hypochondriacal phobia about both his personal health and safety and that of his family and friends. His wife Mary's long siege with diabetes, aggravated by a heart condition that caused her death at the age of fifty-seven in 1983, gave Iacocca compassion for ailing and stricken associates, belying the notion that he is smug and callous.

Father Nick Iacocca started one of the country's first car rental agencies, "U-Drive-It," in the mid-1920s, earning enough money to launch his first real estate venture. Ford cars were Nick's most popular rental make. Years later, it was a Ford that Lee drove back and forth from his parents' brick row house in Allentown to nearby Lehigh University.

That Iacocca holds both a bachelor's and a master's degree in engineering still surprises many auto executives who recall his career as being strictly marketing- and sales-oriented. Lee was graduated with a B.S. in engineering in 1945 from Lehigh, which cited him "with high honors" in recognition of a 3.53 grade-point average, and Iacocca has been quick to point to his engineering achievements when the issue arises in new-product development. His Princeton University master's degree in mechanical engineering makes him an Ivy Leaguer in name if not in spirit.

In 1946, shortly after graduating from Lehigh, Lee applied to a fifty-man training program at Ford. He was told that the program would still be available after he finished at Princeton. However, a new executive was on hand when Iacocca reapplied. The original "promise" had been forgotten, but in typical Iacocca fashion he talked his way into a fifty-first opening and went off to Dearborn. Iacocca regards "self-confidence—belief in ourselves" as the most important value of all. "The symbols mean nothing if the values aren't there," he declares.

At first, Iacocca was assigned to Ford's clutch spring department. After all, the young trainee was a graduate engineer and should have fit into the nuts-and-bolts world like a hand into a glove. But Lee soon found himself at loose ends, bored by the tech life. He left Dearborn and returned to Allentown, but he kept his yen to work for Ford.

As luck would have it, Ford was looking for a truck salesman at its Chester, Pennysylvania, office. The executive in charge of hiring the salesman was Ford sales veteran C. R. Beacham, a Georgia native who was attracted to Iacocca because of his engineering qualifications, and hired him. An engineer hawking heavy-duty trucks to knowledgeable buyers would be a combination too good to pass up.

Iacocca proved such a successful truck peddler that he soon added cars to his portfolio. He was as much a whiz at selling the product then as he is now. He secretly taped a salesman's pitch and played it back before an evening training course to show pluses and minuses. He took one Pennsylvania dealer's entire stock of used cars and personally canvassed the neighborhood, using registration lists to find the owners of the oldest cars, who might be at the point of trading in. The inventory was cleared out in three weeks.

Iacocca describes Beacham as his role model: he could be tough as nails with a Southerner's charm. He pushed Iacocca, who quickly became a zone sales manager in the mid-Atlantic district, to reach for higher and higher volume totals.

"Make money" was Beacham's advice to his aspiring young zone manager. "Screw everything else. This is a profit-making system, boy. The rest is frills."

Early on, Beacham rated Iacocca as a junior executive who went beyond the call of duty on his rounds. But at the same time he chided Iacocca for making excuses if sales fell short of the goals that the factory assigned. As Iacocca recalls it, Beacham, who knew all the alibis, bluntly told him to look in the mirror when he fouled up. In a foretaste of things to come, Iacocca adopted most of Beacham's tough-as-nails approach to underlings. No excuses, and if you can't face the music, good-bye Charlie.

In 1956, when postwar sales finally had slowed down after the pent-up consumer demand had been met, Ford headquarters was looking for a sales gimmick. After an ill-conceived safety campaign floundered (Iacocca tried dropping eggs from a ladder on dismantled "padded" dashboards, but the eggs cracked), Iacocca, undaunted, came up with the slogan "$56 a month for a '56 Ford" for his Philadelphia district dealers. The line caught the attention of Robert McNamara, then Ford division general manager, later Ford president and President John Kennedy's secretary of defense.

Ford adopted the slogan nationwide, and the name of that "Beacham boy" from Pennsylvania, Lee Iacocca, was a household word in Ford headquarters.

At the Ford regional office in Chester, Lee met Mary McCleary, the office receptionist. A romance grew, and the Iacoccas were married when he was promoted to the district sales office in Washington. It wasn't long before Dearborn beckoned, thanks to Charlie Beacham.

As Iacocca acknowledges, having a mentor like Beacham and being in the right place at the right time didn't hurt his fast-moving career. But it wasn't all luck and Beacham's appreciation. In his early stint on the Atlantic seaboard, from Norfolk to Jacksonville, he picked up some of the elements of behavior that helped mold his managerial style.

First off, he took Beacham's advice to use "Lee" with the Southern dealers and salesmen—not "Lido" or the nearly unpronounceable (for them) "Iacocca." Then he ordered his own local staffers to call on both weak sales dealers and volume producers. Lee demanded weekly lists of those dealers to be called upon, and personally checked the results at the beginning of the following week to note any improvements from the poorer-performing dealers.

This led to the concept of periodic review, which Iacocca would install later throughout Ford and at Chrysler. Iacocca firmly believes in a quarterly review by bosses of their staffers' performance, explaining that he has never discovered a better way "to stimulate fresh approaches to problem-solving."

Iacocca credits Charlie Beacham for teaching him how to handle people. Iacocca says he has little use for aspiring executives who, according to their immediate superiors, possess little or no ability to get along with other employees.

A basic Iacocca yardstick, acquired from Beacham, was to exact at least a hundred percent dedication from underlings. E. F. (Gar) Laux, a close Ford sales associate of Iacocca's who later followed him to Chrysler, says that both trainer Beacham and student Iacocca were "ruthless" when it came to the work ethic. "Lee," Laux says, "would bust your ass if he thought you could do it or could do it better. He won't fool around with you if he doesn't feel you've got it. If he's really through with you, he'll almost ignore you."

Laux himself recalls that Beacham, who as assistant general manager of Ford division brought both Iacocca and Laux to Dearborn on the same day in November 1956, was toughest on his top achievers. Beacham once chewed out Laux so savagely that Gar bristled and started to leave Beacham's office after asserting, "I don't have to take that from anybody."

Beacham called Laux back and said, "If I didn't think you had it in you, I wouldn't give you the damn time of day. Now get the hell out of here."

It was a scenario that Iacocca himself reenacted with staffers many times. Like father Nick, like father-figure Charlie, so son Lee.

2

SHAPING UP

THE TROOPS

B
Y DECEMBER 1960, AT THE AGE OF THIRTY-
six, Iacocca had performed so admirably on
the Ford division sales executive track that
he was promoted to the position of general
manager of the division—then as now the second-
highest-volume seller of new cars in the United
States.

The aggressive Iacocca, never one to hide his
light under a bushel, saw the Ford division assignment as a golden opportunity to put into practice a
number of unique management approaches. If they
were successful, Ford might achieve its elusive goal
of surpassing Chevrolet in new-car sales, and Iacocca

would be in a position to rise even further in Ford corporate ranks and responsibilities.

If unsuccessful, Iacocca's "brilliant career" at Ford could be aborted. Company Chairman Henry Ford II lost McNamara to the Kennedy Cabinet in late 1960 and reluctantly advanced a non-product-oriented finance executive, Arjay Miller, to the company presidency to replace him. Miller and Iacocca were not birds of a feather in terms of management philosophy, Miller being more a conservative General Motors type and Iacocca, of course, a pusher and hustler almost without equal in the automotive spectrum. To an Arjay Miller, who later became Ford's vice-chairman and remained on Ford's board of directors, an Iacocca who flubbed up could become a company liability. And Iacocca, who knew his enemies as well as his friends, was fully aware of the personal risks.

But Lee, in command of the Ford division, was not one to shrink from danger at this turn of events. After all, his secret career plan had called for him to reach the top of the divisional heap by 1959, not 1960. At thirty-five years of age, that is—the minimum age for President of the United States!

Iacocca says that when Henry the Deuce, as he is called, gave him the divisional helm to steer, it was the first prolonged talk about business the two had held in all of Iacocca's fourteen years with Ford Motor Company. There weren't many more to follow, according to Iacocca, who implies that he frowns on chief executive officers being so detached that they see senior officers only at executive committee or board of directors meetings. Aloofness is not Lee's style, to say the least, and no one who worked for him at Ford or Chrysler can say that he or she was hired, promoted, penalized, given a raise, or sacked by a third party or in a letter.

The brash Iacocca had a big problem to overcome when he took over Ford division. He was far younger than nearly all his executives. Here again, the counsel of Charlie Beacham on supervising and motivating pulled him through and won him respect from the older hands. Ford's campaign to "beat Chevrolet" in sales—a mission that actually proved to be attainable in only one model year—had the effect of knitting the troops together under the banner held aloft, Henry V–style, by Prince Lee.

And like Shakespeare's Henry V, who led the British against the French in the Bard's most chauvinistic drama, Iacocca assembled a staff of loyalists at the division level. The idea was to pose an Iacocca bloc against any corporate clique—politics of the crassest type on the one hand but smart strategy on the other. The Iacocca gang, moreover, was not composed of lightweights. It included Harold Sperlich, the product developer who preceded Iacocca to Chrysler and who is now Chrysler's president; John Nevin, who later became chairman first of Zenith and later of Firestone Tire and Rubber; and Donald Frey, who succeeded Iacocca to the Ford division general managership and who is now chairman of Bell & Howell.

The luck that Iacocca admits helped his career move upward wasn't merely confined to McNamara's defection to the U.S. government, leaving him free to upgrade McNamara's conservative product and merchandising concepts. Ford had stumbled through the most embarrassing flop in automotive history in the late 1950s when the mid-size Edsel fizzled on the launching pad like a wet firecracker. Iacocca disclaimed any responsiblity, and in truth he had none, but Ford was desperate to erase the fallout from the fiasco and in large measure turned to Iacocca to rejuvenate the company's fortunes and morale.

McNamara, never a champion of pizzazz in cars, had presided over the 1960 launch of the "plain jane" Falcon compact car as an entrant against the new Chevrolet Corvair, Plymouth Valiant, and Volkswagen Beetle models. The Falcon got off to a brisk start, thanks to Iacocca's sales and merchandising campaigns, selling more than 417,000 in its first year. It was a happy omen for Iacocca's recent ascent to the captaincy of Ford division and presaged the development of the spinoff sports coupe that in 1964 topped even Falcon's first-year sales—the celebrated Mustang.

At Ford division, Iacocca inherited the legacy of strong internal financial controls that Miller and Ford's long-time executive vice-president for finance

J. Edward Lundy had rigidly maintained. Ford's fiscal system had been a shambles under Henry Ford I, and it was a paradox to many Iacocca watchers that the wheeling-dealing promotion ace adhered so religiously to what some might regard as a straitjacket.

Actually, however, the finance staff at Ford throughout the Iacocca years, which were from 1946 to 1978, never exerted the hammerlock on administration and executive power widely attributed to the General Motors "bean counters." Four of GM's last five chairmen and chief executive officers, up to and including Roger B. Smith, had previously served as executive vice-presidents of finance. Ed Lundy, an original Ford "whiz kid," never was considered a serious candidate for promotion, although he certainly played a key role in Ford's executive policy-making.

At Ford division, Iacocca coupled the establishment of a palace guard of loyal executives with the development of the "black book" system of vigil over all senior and junior executives. Lee got his reputation for total awareness of every staffer's performance on the job through his own black book on the executives reporting directly to him. They in turn were to keep tabs on their own underlings. The black book approach, as sinister as it sounds, actually flowed from Lee's belief that "if you can't grade a man, you can't follow him at all."

This technique, constantly grading and reviewing, was linked to a requirement for setting and meeting quarterly goals: the review system that he had put into place when he was a regional sales manager. Iacocca ordered each senior executive to set goals for the coming quarter at the time of reviewing results for the previous quarter. Each executive, who went through the same routine for his staff members, was asked to set priorities on the goals—raising truck sales, increasing market share, exceeding Chevrolet in sales, cutting owner warranty claims, and so forth.

Every first-of-the-quarter week came to be known as "crunch time" around Ford because Iacocca was not an easy boss to con. He wanted to know why warranty costs went unreduced or glove boxes kept rattling. If the executive on the firing line blamed someone else, Iacocca asked why the problem hadn't been communicated. If the executive admitted guilt, Lee raised hell and asked the errant Fordnik to re-assess his goals for the next quarter. Opines Iacocca, in no way contrite over treatment that gave a number of otherwise-proud Ford officials quarterly attacks of panic: "If he's a good manager, four times a year he's got to come into the barrel and report. Sometimes they can't wait to tell you because they knocked hell out of what they were going to do. They can't wait to tell you because they know it'll get them a raise...and it will."

It took Iacocca four or five years to shape up the Ford organization under his hardnosed managerial system. One marketing executive, now with a major domestic automaker as a vice-president, left Ford not because the system was wrong but because he felt Iacocca used the power dictatorially to punish men the Iacoccaites disliked. "Review became arrogance," he adds.

In defense of the review system, Iacocca insists that it raises the incidence of self-accountability among department managers. "The discipline of writing something down is the first step toward making it happen": the Chrysler chairman says he learned this from McNamara. Iacocca lists five positive results of quarterly review:

1. It forces a dialogue between the boss and the managers, improving teamwork even between executives who may not like each other.

2. It raises the superior's awareness of praiseworthy performers who could become lost in a big organization and brings deadwood into the open for accountability.

3. Managers walk away feeling that they are their own boss with individualized goals—"in charge" and not a boss's flunky or gofer.

4. Managers become more productive as self-motivation increases.

5. "I've never found a better way to stimulate fresh approaches to problem-solving or to generation of new ideas."

Critics of employee review, led by product-quality guru W. Edwards Deming, who has advised automakers extensively in recent years, find the system counterproductive. "No one wants to help a fellow employee because that guy might get a better review than you," Deming points out.

Entrenchment of the review system at Ford explains in part why Iacocca later recruited so many Ford executives for Chrysler, resulting in the termination of all but three holdover vice-presidents in the previous Chrysler management structure. Ford's defectors to Chrysler, led by Sperlich and Gerald Greenwald (now Chrysler's vice-chairman) were thoroughly committed to the review system, whereas the Chrysler men whom they and their Ford peers replaced were accustomed to running their own "empires" with negligible review by superiors, if any.

Iacocca also believed that man for man (no women were then involved) his old Ford cronies were superior to their predecessors at Chrysler. One displaced veteran Chrysler engineering executive tried to adapt to the new system of "reporting" and "reviewing" under Iacocca, but he found it too difficult to follow for himself or enforce on his junior engineers. Yet this executive had, together with Sperlich, brought close to development many of the restyled front-wheel-drive products that had helped save Chrysler—the compact K-cars, the revolutionary minivans, and the Omni and Horizon subcompacts.

Typically, Iacocca finally fired the unadaptable executive, though the successor he appointed was not a Ford refugee but the man's chief assistant at Chrysler, who proved to be more capable of fitting in. Not even Iacocca, who makes a fetish of loyalty, would question the review system's value as an ego massager for superiors who may need it from quarter to quarter.

As any emperor or imperious chief executive officer knows, fear of confrontation with the boss also can be pivotal in separating the winners from the losers. Iacocca has discovered that his modus operandi unearths misplaced managers who voluntarily ask for reassignment after "flunking" several quarterly review sessions. "I hate the job, please relieve me," Iacocca says these misfits plead. "And we do. It's better than firing him."

Is the review system infallible? The approach fits in like a synchromesh transmission where automotive manufacturing, sales, purchasing, and engineering operations are concerned. Fixed goals are to be met; owner complaints are to be satisfied. Costs are either reduced or kept from increasing above a certain percentage. But Iacocca admits that review is a far less definable concept in public relations, labor relations, or advertising.

In these areas, where the bottom line well may be the top line in terms of procompany benefits, Iacocca relies on finding capable and trusted vice-presidents who are strong leaders themselves. At

Ford, his public relations confidant was Walter Murphy, who engineered many of the successful product introductions, such as the 1964 Mustang, which redounded to the benefit of both the company and Iacocca personally. (Murphy chose to retire when Iacocca left Ford, declining an offer to sign on at Chrysler.) Chrysler's public affairs and public relations are supervised by two men who came from competitors, James L. Tolley and Baron K. Bates, respectively, and their ideas have played a major role in transforming the Chrysler image so dramatically. Unlike most of Chrysler's other vice-presidents, curiously, neither Tolley nor Bates ever worked with Lee at Ford.

Communicating is nothing if not Iacocca's forte—and he takes a dim view of executives who at their quarterly review sessions complain about the media or shrink from press contacts. It is significant in Iacocca's scheme of things that for the area of communications, he turned to two careerists from outside the Ford group who had shared years of automotive know-how. Where better to find new PR chiefs for a Chrysler whose public image was zero than at competitive automakers that had excelled in the public awareness arena—the number-one auto-selling division, Chevrolet, and Volkswagen, with its 1960s and early 1970s cult car, the rear-engine Beetle?

In the touchy area of labor relations, one breakthrough by Iacocca marked a radical departure for all of American industry: He invited United Auto Workers President Douglas Fraser to serve on the Chrysler board of directors in 1980—a precedent-breaker that many observers feel paved the way for upgrading the quality of Chrysler products because the Chrysler workers felt they had a voice in corporate management for the first time. It didn't hurt Chrysler, which really had nothing to lose, that Fraser was an articulate and knowledgeable union leader with few internal enemies and without any hang-ups about rubbing shoulders with management fat cats. Fraser's retirement as UAW president in 1983 raised questions about whether Chrysler would retain a UAW "seat" on its board, since his successor as president of the union, the doughty Owen F. Bieber, seemed to lack Fraser's sophistication and appeal to the Chrysler rank-and-file. But after Fraser had served on the board for a fourth year, and Bieber led the UAW in completion of new three-year contracts with relatively modest cost increases, Bieber took his place as a Chrysler director and kept intact an Iacocca idea that had now become a Chrysler policy.

Asked about Iacocca in January 1985, the astute Fraser made an observation that puts into perspective the Chrysler chairman's management persona quite aptly: "When he makes a Chrysler decision, he fully expects it to be carried out retroactively." Then, asked if Iacocca were a benevolent-dictator type, Fraser replied with tongue in cheek: "Strike the word benevolent."

Iacocca's greatest product success at Ford, the 1964 Mustang, reflected both the fine-tuning of the personnel review system and the product instincts of Iacocca himself. The cream rose to the top in both cases, resulting in a sales winner and a new product with which Iacocca remains indelibly connected.

The Mustang was spawned by the consumer upgrading of Ford's Falcon econocar, which arrived in the early 1960s in consort with Chevrolet's rear-engine Corvair and Chrysler Corporation's Plymouth Valiant. Iacocca found as head of Ford division that suddenly Falcon buyers wanted more than bare bones. They were looking for peppier engines and automatic transmissions, not to mention whitewall tires and air conditioning.

Why not, Iacocca asked his product group, jazz up the Falcon with a sporty coupe model, seating up to four and appealing to an upscale market? It took two and one-half years to bring the Mustang to fruition—in time for a typical Iacocca introduction splash at the New York World's Fair of 1964.

The new Mustang had unprecedented immediate sales acceptance. It had been so avidly promoted by Iacocca's Ford staffers that nearly four million people visited Ford dealerships to see it in April 1964, and Iacocca's picture adorned the covers *both* of *Time* and *Newsweek*.

Mustang's debut sales kept pyramiding. Iacocca soon discarded his cautious goal of 75,000 deliveries, adding assembly points as fast as possible and finally winding up with a record first-year volume of 417,174 cars by mid-April 1965.

In its initial two years on the market, the hot little Mustang generated net profits for Ford of $1.1 billion—no small amount in those days. The long-hooded, short-decked Mustang became Iacocca's golden chariot, his success symbol, his first claim to fame (although many at Ford who contributed to the Mustang's birth resented what they considered his failure to share credit for the accomplishment).

It's worthy of note that the chairman's office at Chrysler has exhibited on occasion a sculpted early Mustang scale model or a photograph of Iacocca with a 1964 original, one of which he still proudly owns.

It has often been said that a corporation is not a democracy and cannot be successfully run like one. This question arises about the review system and the black books: Are they the trappings of a corporate czar who would like to be assured at least every quarter that his subjects love him, since they can't vote on his reelection? Or are they a way of amassing loyalty through "creative fear"? Or are they rather a neglected system that should be emulated by other businesses, big and small? Suffice it to say that at two major automaking companies that had been in deep trouble, it worked as an innovative management process; its strongest advocate is Lee Iacocca.

3

CHRYSLER: FROM CREST TO CRISIS

THE HISTORY OF CHRYSLER CORPORATION IS laced with peaks and valleys, strong managers and weak ones, scintillating profit years and horrendous losses. Chrysler was a shambles when Iacocca took charge in 1979, but it had been a formidable competitor in its day and had fought back from the terminally ill ward time and again.

Unlike Ford, which Iacocca already knew, Chrysler was structured more as a medieval kingdom ruled by one man and encompassing fiefdoms that were led in turn by tyrannical crown princes. For example, whoever ran engineering, always a power at Chrysler, reported only to the chairman. It was the same with finance, sales, and manufacturing. At Ford, the various group or staff vice-presidents reported through executive vice-presidents to Iacocca, who finally became company president in December 1970. Iacocca's upward mobility had been interrupted by Chairman Henry Ford's installation of former General Motors Executive Vice-President Semon E. (Bunkie) Knudsen as Ford president in 1968. Ford let Knudsen go and promoted Iacocca after telling the GM "outsider" that "things just aren't working out." (Iacocca has never denied speculation that he and his loyal teammates in Ford's upper echelons kept Knudsen from functioning as effectively as he might have liked.) The organization from which Knudsen came, GM, used the "committee system" in an attempt, not always successful, to reach consensus decisions for approval by the chairman and president.

A review of Chrysler's history shows why the monarchy-duchy system, so dependent on the whims of the men in command, endured almost as many traumas as triumphs in the fifty-three years before Iacocca moved in.

Chrysler had been founded by a hard-driving executive who matriculated into the automotive business through a competitive automaker, as Iacocca did. Walter Percy Chrysler was his name, and he too had been widely credited with saving corporations when disaster threatened.

Walter Chrysler grew up in the small Kansas

towns of Wamego and Ellis. His father was a passenger train engineer, and early on Walter developed a passion for machines. At the age of seventeen, in 1891, he determined to become a machinist and, upon graduation from high school, went to work as a railroad shop sweeper, eventually becoming a full-fledged machinist. In 1908, the year when Henry Ford introduced the Model T and William C. Durant organized GM, Chrysler became a superintendent for the Chicago Great Western Railway.

When Chrysler, who did not even know how to drive, happened to visit a Chicago automobile show, he became enamored of an ivory-white Locomobile that had red leather upholstery, brass trim, and a khaki top. The car cost five thousand dollars and, although Chrysler was only earning $350 a month, he swung a bank loan with help from a cosigning friend. The Locomobile was shipped to Chrysler, who proceeded to take it apart and put it back together again several times. It was this experience that turned Chrysler's ambition toward becoming an auto builder himself, although he first joined Pittsburgh's American Locomotive Company as a works manager.

By 1910, the flamboyant Durant had nearly bankrupted General Motors because of loan over-extensions. James J. Storrow, who was chairman of GM's finance committee and also a director of American Locomotive, was seeking to create a new management team for GM. Storrow asked Chrysler to leave the railroad business and join Charles Nash at GM's Buick division as works manager, even though the move would mean a pay cut. Chrysler jumped at the chance.

When Chrysler, then thirty-six, came to the Buick complex in Flint, Michigan, production had been slashed to only forty-five cars a day. By contrast, Ford was assembling a thousand cars a day. Chrysler, an innovator, scrapped the traditonal carriage-making assembly method and established moving production lines, copying techniques introduced at GM's Cadillac division as well as at Ford. By demanding engineering proficiency, he got Buick back on its feet, so that by 1915 its sales had risen to 140,000 cars a year.

In another parallel with later automaker "saviors," Chrysler asked GM President Charley Nash (after whom the Nash car was later named) for an "or-else" raise to $25,000 in 1915 and $50,000 in 1916. Nash acquiesced. After Durant then regained control of GM and forced Nash out, Nash asked Chrysler to join him in establishing Nash Motors in Kenosha, Wisconsin. But Durant prevailed upon Chrysler to stay aboard GM's ship with an offer of the presidency of Buick, then GM's top profit division, at a salary of $500,000 a year. Chrysler also became vice-president in charge of manufacturing operations for GM.

Chrysler found Durant to be a tough boss who liked yes-men and went his own way more often than not. Conflicts between the two men escalated during World War I. In 1919, aged forty-five, Chrysler "retired" a millionaire. But he could not resist the opportunity to return to the auto business as a way of building his own car.

The postwar slump threatened to wipe out the Willys-Overland and Maxwell Motor Car companies. Chrysler came to the rescue, induced by the firms' bankers to help save them both. Chrysler's bailout work for Willys brought him into contact with a trio of consulting engineers—Fred M. Zeder, Carl Breer, and Owen R. Skelton—who helped in the Willys reorganization and who impressed Chrysler as technicians with a preoccupation with quality.

The Zeder-Breer-Skelton team, later to be known as Chrysler's "three musketeers," turned out to be just what Chrysler was looking for to start his own company. They went to work for him at Maxwell, developing an innovative medium-priced car that was to be introduced at the New York Automobile Show in January 1924 as the "Chrysler Six." It featured a high-compression engine plus hydraulic brakes, replaceable oil filters, aluminum pistons, and shock absorbers—all components that had been confined to higher-priced cars.

The debut of the Chrysler Six produced results that astounded the industry. The high-flying "Roaring Twenties" were in full swing, but no first-year car had ever collected 32,000 orders. The Chrysler

Six did exactly that, and Walter P. plunged ahead with plans to kick off Chrysler Corporation, to be headquartered in Highland Park, an enclave city surrounded by Detroit.

Soon after Chrysler was officially formed, a second car was announced: the Chrysler Four, in four body styles. The Four introduced a technological first: isolation of the engine from the frame, with the use of springs and bushes to reduce vibration. In 1926 came the first Chrysler Imperial for the luxury market and also the four-cylinder Chrysler 50, boasting a top speed of fifty miles per hour and fuel economy of twenty miles per gallon.

During 1926, with the United States in the midst of a headlong growth cycle, the new Chrysler Corporation built 129,565 vehicles, compared with Ford's 1,137,181 (the classic Model T was still a brisk seller, although its demise was near) and General Motors' 892,007. GM outsold Ford for the first time in 1927, forcing a reluctant Henry Ford II to authorize in 1928 the introduction of the Model A. Ford regained the sales lead over GM in the first Model A years, but GM eventually won back the supremacy which it has not relinquished to this day. The GM drive for leadership under prudent financial expert Alfred P. Sloan, Jr. added greatly to the challenges facing Chrysler, which had come into being as an entrant basically in the low-priced segment dominated by Ford. It was incumbent upon Chrysler that it broaden its market coverage.

By 1927, Chrysler had become the fourth-largest automaker in the United States. Walter Chrysler, as chief executive officer, was assembling a team of experts to work with the "three musketeers." His finance man was hardnosed Bernice Edwin Hutchinson, who was always known as "B.E." A former GM production associate, Kaufman Thuma Keller ("K.T.") came on board to head up manufacturing. The crucial dealer organization was the domain of Abe VanderZee.

The year 1928 was a banner year for Chrysler in terms of taking on both of its two major competitors. Walter Chrysler purchased the Dodge Brothers' auto company in Hamtramck, next door to Highland Park, which boasted a solid dealer organization and came with a forge and a foundry, which Chrysler lacked and whose products Chrysler had been compelled to buy outside at higher costs. Dodge also had a truck plant, which rounded out Chrysler's motor vehicle mix. Dodge trucks, sold by the Dodge dealers along with cars, were highly regarded performers that more often than not weathered business downturns that slashed car sales. At the same time, Chrysler unveiled both the Plymouth car, in the low-priced arena of the market, and the DeSoto, as a contender between the Chrysler Six and the newly acquired Dodge in the upper-medium segment.

This lineup of cars—Chrysler, Dodge and Plymouth—continues to form the gut structure of Chrysler's product offerings. The DeSoto was dropped in the 1961 model year after it had become too close to the top-of-the-line Chrysler in price and image, although it was a profit generator for the corporation for most of its thirty-three years.

Today, with Chrysler's $1.7 billion cash hoard as of January 1, 1985, acquisition prospects of a Chrysler-Dodge type are hard to come by, although Iacocca is not an unwilling suitor. He proposed a merger in 1982 with West Germany's Volkswagen-werk auto corporation, but the VW board thought Chrysler too risky a partner. Ironically, Chrysler subsequently was to take over a VW-owned plant outside Detroit in Sterling Heights, Michigan, where production of the new Chrysler LeBaron GTS and Dodge Lancer sports sedans began late in 1984. (VW may have thought the Sterling Heights plant sale to Chrysler a turnabout twist because of the fact that the New Stanton, Pennsylvania, plant site, where it assembles Golf subcompact cars, was originally acquired from ... Chrysler!)

John and Horace Dodge, like Walter Chrysler, had grown up in a small town and were trained as machinists. Having moved to Detroit, the brothers opened a machine shop that supplied transmissions for Oldsmobile and helped Henry Ford redesign the powertrain for his new Model T car. In 1903, Ford signed up the Dodge shop as an engine supplier in exchange for 100 of Ford's newly issued 1000 shares. The Dodges paid for their 10 percent equity with $3000 in cash and $7000 in materials. Eleven years later, after a heated row with "Mr. Ford," the temperamental Dodges sold out for $25 million and organized their own company to build a car priced about $100 above the Model T.

The first auto-company proving grounds were built by the Dodges, whose car quickly achieved a reputation for reliability. This in turn helped draw in a solid dealer organization, many members of which had been "burned" by the fickle performance of many of the new cars launched in pre–World War I years. The Dodge brothers died a year apart during the 1920 influenza epidemic and left the company to their widows. The value of the company at that time was estimated at $52 million.

The Dodge widows kept control of the company for five years of America's postwar boom, during which almost anything on four wheels was salable. They picked up the Graham Brothers truckmaking plant during that period, thereby giving Dodge car dealers a highly profitable truck franchise. In 1925, the Dodge widows sold out to the New York investment banking firm of Dillon, Read for $146 million.

Not automakers, Dillon, Read decided on a quick-buck strategy to recoup their investment. The Dodge car was gussied up with extras, and the price was doubled by 1928 to $1500, as against $495 for Ford's Model A. Sales plunged, and Clarence Dillon sought out Walter Chrysler, who had written of his avid interest in the "splendid plants of Dodge." Chrysler agreed to buy Dodge for about $170 million.

This single purchase made Chrysler the third largest U.S. automaker overnight. The combined assets of Chrysler and Dodge amounted to $260 million. Chrysler grew with that one fell swoop into an eighteen-plant company capable of building up to one million cars and trucks a year. It was also a period of vast dealer organizations, and the combined Chrysler-Dodge total of about twelve thousand retail outlets was three times greater than the present-day count.

The Dodge purchase, in retrospect, shored up Chrysler in terms of market coverage and cost reduction to such an extent that it enabled Chrysler to survive the Great Depression of the 1930s, the World War II period, which almost sank Ford, and the recessions of the late 1950s and mid-1970s.

Iacocca, a master at introducing new cars, would have appreciated the glitz with which the low-priced Plymouth was unveiled in 1928 at New York's Madison Square Garden. Famed aviatrix Amelia Earhart accompanied the new Plymouth at its debut. The car itself was advertised as representative of "the endurance, strength and rugged honesty of the American Pilgrims."

With the company growing almost like topsy on one hand, Walter Chrysler at the same time denied any objective of "straining after domination" or seeking "to attain mere size or volume." He insisted that the company's business was being "built step by step in relation to the capacities of the nation and of the industry as a whole." There were disbelievers on Wall Street, but the later K. T. Keller regime also steered clear of the Chevrolet-Ford sales position or penetration. Chrysler executives after Keller were to shun the founder's pronouncement about corporate ambitions, mindful of the need to stir their dealers with share-of-market (penetration) or volume targets.

But Chrysler was not above grandiose and precedent-breaking moves that served to stimulate business. The Plymouth, instead of getting its own dealer organizations, was sold through existing Chrysler, DeSoto, and Dodge dealers. This worked like a charm in the first three years of the Depression, and by 1932 the four-cylinder Plymouth, priced at $600, had won 14 percent of the low-priced market away from the seemingly entrenched Chevy and Ford. A radically designed sloping-shape car, the Chrysler Airflow, was introduced in 1934 and, while it proved to be a catastrophic flop in terms of public acceptance, it established Chrysler's reputation as an automaker willing to take risks and break traditions.

In 1936, Chrysler was completely debt-free, with a market share of a lusty 25 percent. (The Chrysler share sank as low as 8 percent in 1981 and reached 12 percent in 1984.) The Depression had left Chrysler stronger instead of weaker, although many smaller automakers were biting the dust because of swollen inventories of unsalable cars. Chrysler ran into this problem at first, but then it instituted a rigidly enforced system of building *only* to dealer orders. Iacocca himself reverted to this practice at Chrysler in 1980, ending the self-destructive "sales bank" production policy practiced by his predecessors.

In 1935, Walter Chrysler stepped down from the presidency (he remained chairman until his death in 1940) and promoted K. T. Keller to the position. Keller, a stout and strong-minded manufacturing expert, was Chrysler's personal choice, winning the nod over the finance chief, B. E. Hutchinson, and the engineering boss, Fred Zeder. Chrysler was drawn to Keller because both were poor boys who had become successful, Horatio Alger—style. They had met at Buick, where Keller was master mechanic. He rose to manufacturing vice-president of Chevrolet before joining Chrysler in 1926 at the personal request of Walter P. himself.

Keller was the dominant figure at Chrysler for twenty-one years but, dramatically unlike his mentor, he became a resister of corporate or product innovation. While Chrysler's big and small competitors greeted the post—World War II years with such advances as Studebaker's glass-encased Starlite coupe, the "stepdown" Hudson, and Chevrolet's lightweight V-8 engine, Chrysler clung to prewar designs and management systems. Like changes brought about later, up to and including the advent of Iacocca and his Ford team, Chrysler's "Forward

Look" new cars of the mid-1950s came years later than competition.

A hallmark of Keller's presidency and chairman-ship at Chrysler was his involvement in every area of company business, maintaining the "strong man" tradition left by Walter Chrysler and bequeathed, for better or worse, to all future Chrysler chief exec-utives. One analyst in the early 1950s called Chrys-ler's organization the equivalent of a rimless wheel. Departmental or divisional spokes all flowed from Keller at the hub. Only he could see what everyone was doing.

Lacking corporate executive vice-presidents with authority over the Dodge and Chrysler divisional presidents and the engineering and marketing vice-presidents, Chrysler under Keller developed tunnel vision, born out of past financial and sales triumphs. Keller involved himself personally in rearranging new plant tools, and in approving all ads. He also accepted the conservative fiscal philosophy of finance vice-president Hutchinson, who argued that Chrysler's profits should be used mainly to increase shareholder dividends and executive salaries, spending only what was necessary to maintain and increase production.

Until his retirement in 1953, "Hutch" was the power behind the throne at Chrysler. The dealer organization of the sales vice-president VanderZee carried the U.S. mail in the early postwar years and were rated among the best of any in the industry.

So why rock the boat? Hutch and his chairman, K.T., would have screamed and hollered (literally— they were tough men who spoke their minds bluntly and treated the media like pariahs) at any under- lings who suggested more than a token outlay for spending on new product development. (By con- trast, after Chrysler's record earnings in 1984 of $2.4 billion, Iacocca showed how far the company had come in thirty years when he announced plans for spending $10.5 billion on new product devel- opment over the next five years. "That's what we have to do to stay as healthy as we are today," he explained.)

Keller's bluntness—and intransigence—were aptly displayed at a new-model preview in the early 1950s. All other competitive post–World War II models by this time had lowered their rooflines. Chrysler's were as high as ever and Keller, who always wore his hat in the office and insisted on cars with plenty of headroom, was asked why. "We build cars to sit in, not piss over," he replied.

There was a rationale at Chrysler for the resis- tance to updated styling in cars. The reputation for "dependable" vehicles that were soundly engi- neered was overriding, carried over with the Zeder- Skelton-Breer and Dodge Brothers linkages. The corporation frowned on consumer surveys, but it knew that blue-collar workers liked their cars to hold up and disdained jazzy styling. Moreover, the Airflow failure had steered Keller away from use of stylists as more than executors of engineers' concepts. New two-seaters with modern designs from Chevrolet and Ford, the Corvette and Thunderbird, respectively, got the cold shoulder in the 1950s from the powers-that-were at Chrysler. After all, why not ride it out with cars as boxy and high as the prewar models on the heels of record profits that reached $132.2 million in 1949?

But a day of reckoning, the first in Chrysler history, was on the way. Chrysler's 1953 models, actually shortened by Keller's command even though GM and Ford were making their cars longer and wider, suffered an early sales slump. Ford outsold Chrysler for second place for the first time—and never yielded the runner-up position after that. The Korean War ended, and with it the pent-up market for new cars that had continued since 1945.

It was time for a change.

4

TRAILBLAZERS, LEAKS, AND PAYOLA

THAT LEE IACOCCA OF CHRYSLER AND ROGER Smith of GM almost single-handedly revitalized the U.S. auto industry is recognized far and wide. They had vastly different corporations to manage—the one hanging by a thread when Iacocca took command, the other an international giant battered by the early 1980s recession but laden with cash reserves greater than those of most state treasuries.

The main lesson of the Iacocca/Chrysler and Smith/GM eras to date should not be lost on any corporate board of directors: A skillful and innovative chief executive officer is worth his weight in gold; an overly conservative chairman fearful of departing from "precedent" can prove a long-term hardship case, even for a company as omnipotent as GM.

In Iacocca's case, necessity was both the mother and the father of corporate invention. He probably would have insisted on it anyway, but Chrysler's board gave him free rein to beg, borrow, hire, fire, spend, save, launch, or scrap models. Whether Iacocca knew it or not, he became the man with the thumb in the dike. He rose to the occasion in brilliant fashion, conquering not only decades of corporate mismanagement but the deep auto sales recession of the early 1980s and the antibailout inclinations of many powers in Washington and the financial community.

Smith, a GM-trained finance executive who had never headed either a new-car division or a corporate staff that involved itself with manufacturing and product development, chose the path of innovative expansionism, a radical break with the nesting approach of all his predecessors. It is hard to imagine the low-key Thomas A. Murphy, the GM chairman immediately preceding Smith, spending billions to acquire Hughes Aircraft or Electronic Data Systems or establishing a separate $5 billion subsidiary corporation—Saturn—to build a small car like the Japanese. To be sure, the election and reelection of free-enterprise zealot Ronald Reagan as President dampened the antitrust fires that GM often gave as a reason for balking at outside purchases like EDS or joint-venture automaking agreements like that with Toyota in Fremont, California. GM, until Smith, had been content even under Republican administrations in Washington to avoid acquisitions or pioneering potentially revolutionary systems for doing business on the inside.

Iacocca and Smith plunged into unwalked paths for their companies—and succeeded. The feat at Chrysler was engineered by an "outsider" who had nothing to lose except personal pride, in view of Chrysler's plight when he took over. Smith's moves were made, seemingly without the pressure faced by Iacocca, by a GM chairman who realized that GM's long-range future was at risk in a continuing policy of nongrowth. What the two chairmen had achieved by 1985 in their respective ways is certain to be the subject of many graduate business school theses and dissertations in years to come.

Smith, a "futurist" in a job previously held by here-and-now realists at GM, is presiding over a stem-to-stern reorganization that has as a prime focus the conversion of one of the corporate world's classic bureaucracies into an outfit of free-thinkers and even entrepreneurs.

A deceptive personality in that he can sound bubbly in person but possesses a dullish oratorical style, Smith has attained respect bordering on awe from within GM and from the financial community.

"In GM," says William E. Hoglund, president of Saturn Corporation, a GM subsidiary created by Smith to develop and market a small car with radically new production and sales concepts, "the organization had to be reformed to respond to Roger's creative drive."

Thus, instead of following the lead of past GM executives, who would have added Saturn as a unit of Chevrolet or some other existing division, Smith has charged Hoglund with the task of building an autonomous unit that will write its own UAW contract, establish separate dealers, build a 6000-job plant on its own agenda, and possibly sell stock to the public.

"GM now has more creative people expressing their ideas than ever before," declares David Cole, director of the University of Michigan's Office for the Study of Automotive Transportation and the son of a former GM president, the late Edward N. Cole. "Roger has legitimized the idea that change isn't that bad."

Both Iacocca and Smith share intensity and concentration in their own ways, not unlike that seen in a champion tennis player or diver. Such concentration in a leader can be magnetic toward fellow workers, psychologists who study business executives believe, and often accomplish results that others achieve only through coercive methods.

The Chrysler Corporation of 1956, coping with the worst financial crisis in its thirty-two-year history, turned to a Smith-type insider to accomplish an Iacocca-type turnaround. He was Lester Lum ("Tex") Colbert, who since 1950 had champed at the bit as

Chairman Keller's president while Chrysler's outmoded prewar cars languished and the mini-empires
of the division and staff vice-presidents kept doing
their own orbiting. When Keller finally retired that
year, Colbert, with the chief executive's authority for
the first time, set out to reform the creaking monster
and make it competitive again against GM and Ford.

A brawny six-footer, Tex Colbert shared small-town
roots with Walter Chrysler and K. T. Keller, but little
else. He was voluble and outgoing, whereas they
tended to be secretive and terse. Chrysler's two-man
public relations staff reportedly had worked under
Keller's order to "treat 'em rough and tell 'em nothing," in handling media inquiries even on such mun-
dane and semipublic material as weekly production
statistics. Colbert loosened the reins on Chrysler
public relations, and Iacocca's media affinity is so
pronounced that he even allowed the press to publish
photographs and specifications of years-away models
in his early years as chairman.

No mechanics or finance expert, Colbert brought
to Chrysler a legal background and a flair for the quick
assimilation of matters of a technical nature for which
he had not been trained. A Harvard Law School graduate, he started his career at Chrysler's law firm in
New York and so impressed Walter Chrysler that he
was asked to start an in-house legal department at
headquarters in Detroit.

The parallels between the Colbert and Iacocca stories are amazingly similar. Both men were quick

learners of all things automotive, though one was a lawyer and the other an engineer; both had flamboyant and even domineering personalities, small-town roots, and Ivy League graduate degrees; and both were inheritors of the Chrysler steering wheel at times of great company stress.

But the similarities end with the moment after coronation. Colbert set about in a massive way to reform Chrysler's entrenched modus operandi—and failed. He tried to implement consultant recommendations for management decentralization and de-emphasis of the powerful engineering department, but resistance by the hostile bureaucracy was so adamant that Colbert made an about-face by 1957 and ordered "recentralization." By contrast, twenty-five years later, Iacocca hacked away at the establishment as a sine qua non for Chrysler's survival. Lee stuck to his guns, whereas Tex gave up when the going got tough; he was inclined to settle out of court rather than risk a jury's verdict that might have given him total victory. Had Colbert prevailed and strengthened Chrysler as the 1960s approached, Iacocca might have found no weakened automaker to save in the United States after his ouster from Ford.

By 1958, Colbert had made next to no strides in changing Chrysler's internal Keller-Zeder management structure, but he at least had debuted longer and more trend-setting new cars with rear fender fins, conceived by the company's first vice-president for styling, Virgil Exner. The finned look is gauche by today's styling standards, but the 1957 public liked the "flight-sweep" cars, and the domestic competitors were quick to follow suit. Colbert pressed Chrysler dealers to reach a goal he had set in 1954 — 20 percent of the market nationally and locally — foreshadowing the pressure-the-dealer syndrome that later helped bring the company to near-ruin. Sales did improve, at least until GM and Ford caught up with the outlandish fins, but another tack Colbert pursued as a profit-bolstering device subsequently was to hurt Chrysler even more: quicker new-model preparation cycles.

Colbert chopped a full twelve months from Chrysler's normal three-year cycle for launching new cars, aiming to bring in all the 1957 models with the "Forward Look" fins. Production was triggered with less than half of the dies completed. The result: Windows and doors leaked, transmissions broke down, two new engines were scrapped at the starting line, body rustout started the first winter after introduction because of the use of ungalvanized steel. Moreover, the once-carefully-tended dealer body was handed a second chore foreign to its tradition. Colbert had not only asked dealers to regain 20 percent of the market but had asked them to do so with poorly built cars that the dealers had to rewire, tow back from irate customers, and in all too many cases reassemble. It was the all-but-tragic end of a quality reputation that Chrysler had maintained from the beginning in 1924.

Robert B. McCurry, newly hired out of Michigan State University in the mid-1950s as a junior sales executive, later to become sales vice-president at Chrysler, recalls it this way: "I think the No. 1 issue in our company at that time that caused us to make some bad decisions on products was our quality.... I believe that financial people looked at projects and I call it being dollar-wise and penny-foolish or penny-wise and dollar-foolish; and decisions were made from that level.

"Quality became . . . the key issue that caused our problems because we created a lot of unhappy customers. They weren't going to come back and buy another product. That fellow leaning over the fence telling how bad it is sends eight away; and the guy leaning over the fence telling how good it is only brings a couple in.

"So, the whole ballgame caught up with us. And when we had a good economy, Chrysler stayed in there and hung in. When it got bad, we really went down. And then a whole trend developed toward the end. With the emissions and all the government controls and the costs of doing that, it just caught up with them. . . . I blame it on the quality of the product which was brought about by cost decisions."

Marketing expert McCurry was one of a cadre of new men brought into Chrysler management in the 1950s as the wave of the future. Another was the epitome of the cost vigilante, one Lynn Townsend, a certified public accountant who joined the company in 1957 as comptroller. Colbert, realizing that the company was thin in upper-middle management personnel, so-called "bench strength," had set about to recruit replacements in Detroit. But he could not begin to attract the outside talent in the way Iacocca did in the late 1970s and early 1980s. Chrysler's grievous product problems, which came on the heels of a bitter hundred-day UAW strike in 1950 that led to numerous wildcat strikes and continuing fractious labor relations, did not make the number-three automaker a secure environment for an ambitious young engineer or sales manager from GM or Ford.

It was in the 1957–58 period that Chrysler, despite Colbert's stout efforts, first rode the rollercoaster that was to typify its future. The Chrysler chairman, accepting the recommendations of a management consultant group, completed three new assembly plants and purchased an interest in the French automaker Simca. But after the fin-look cars propelled Chrysler to a $125.1 million profit and an 18.3 percent market share in 1957, the bottom fell out in the recession year 1958 as the structural defects of the 1957 models gained widespread public awareness. Chrysler's sales nosedived 50 percent, and the company lost $29.6 million in 1958, which was followed by a $2 million loss in 1959. By 1960, the market share had foundered to a dismal 14 percent. Quality had deteriorated to such an extent that once-loyal Chrysler, Dodge, and Plymouth owners deserted in droves, many not to return until the Iacocca years.

Meanwhile, a radical shift in popular taste toward plain economical cars and away from the glitzy fin look was forcing the Big Three automakers to order quick fixes in their product lineups as the decade of the 1960s approached. The Volkswagen Beetle and the Renault Dauphine were catching on in the United States, boosting 1959 sales of all imported cars to a 10.1 percent share of the total market. In 1960, American Motors, under the inspirational leadership of Chairman George Romney, who two years later would be elected governor of Michigan, elevated sales of a low-priced econocar called the Rambler to 363,000, and Studebaker's Lark, the only domestic competitor to the Rambler, notched 133,000 sales. When Chrysler learned that Chevrolet was developing the rear-engine Corvair and the Ford the "plain jane" Falcon as small-car entries, it hustled to stay with the flow and initiated development of what was to be the 1960 Plymouth Valiant, although the company was in deep financial straits.

Colbert was in the middle of a maelstrom. The ink bath of 1958, accentuated by persistent quality and labor problems as well as the volatile shifts in the marketplace, were troubles enough for any chairman. But Colbert's rule was challenged directly, starting in 1958, when a "gadfly" stockholder, Detroit attorney Sol Dann, launched a crusade against what he called "conflict-of-interest" purchases of materials and services from suppliers in which Chrysler officers had equities.

Although Colbert himself was never linked to any payola, he suffered an irreparable blow when it turned out that his protégé and successor as Chrysler president, William C. Newberg, did own interests in two supplier companies. Newberg, an engineer who had joined Chrysler as a test driver in 1933, had been named Chrysler president on April 28, 1960, only eight months after he and Tex had unveiled the Valiant at Chrysler previews in Miami Beach.

Dann and his associates did a little unveiling of their own and exposed Newberg's "conflict of interest." A special board meeting in New York fired the astounded Newberg sixty-four days later. Colbert reassumed the presidency, but the clouds darkened when Dann filed a series of shareholder suits accusing the company of winking at insider deals between executives and vendors.

Colbert could not continue to run the Chrysler organization, lest whatever credibility the company had left disappear completely. He resigned on July 27, 1961. The Chrysler chairmanship was assumed by a highly regarded outside director, George Love, sixty-one, who headed Pittsburgh's Consolidation Coal and had led an internal Chrysler task force that was designed to clean house in the wake of the Sol Dann revelations.

In a foreshadowing of the overtures made eighteen years later to Iacocca, Love approached two General Motors general managers—Chevrolet's Edward N. Cole and Pontiac's "Bunkie" Knudsen—to become Chrysler president and chief operating officer, respectively. But both knew they were in contention for the presidency of GM and turned Love down. Similarly, Ford division's General Manager Iacocca was urged by some to go after the Chrysler post, but he preferred to stay on track for the Ford presidency. Others gave Love a cold rebuff, adding to Chrysler's sour reputation with the public at large.

Colbert had promoted Lynn Townsend, the ambitious young accountant, to administrative vice-president in 1960. Love now seemingly had no choice but to turn to the finance-oriented Townsend, despite his lack of technical know-how. So in 1961, at the age of forty-two, Townsend was named president of Chrysler with the clear understanding that he would assume the chairmanship from Love in due course. Townsend was described by a Chrysler vice-president who later left the company when he was bypassed for the presidency as "the best man around who would accept the job."

It was a far cry from the way Townsend's successor as chairman, John Riccardo, depicted Iacocca when he hired the ousted Ford president: "He's the best executive in the auto industry. Period."

5

WHO NEEDS

ACCOUNTANTS?

CCOUNTANTS, YES. "SERIOUS FINANCIAL
analysts"—no way. So says Lee Iacocca
of Lynn Townsend and John Riccardo,
who preceded him as chairmen of Chrysler and who shoulder most of the blame for the
deteriorating conditions Iacocca found when he
agreed to join the number-three automaker.

What bothered the Ford-trained Iacocca was that
Chrysler lacked a comprehensive system of financial controls, despite the fact that the finance-
oriented Townsend and his protégé Riccardo had
run the company for eighteen years. Iacocca's diagnosis of what maladies had befallen the once-for-

midable Chrysler reveals much of his management philosophy.

Iacocca acknowledges that he had all but ignored Chrysler while he was a senior executive at Ford. "Ever since Ford had surpassed Chrysler in the early 1950's," he asserts, "all our attention was directed toward General Motors." He had only visited Chrysler headquarters once before assuming the Chrysler presidency, to engage in a Big Three summit meeting on UAW negotiating strategy.

At Ford, every plant operated on a strict budget. The rate of return on investment was a constant financial yardstick for every plant manager, not to mention for every divisional and staff administrator. Yet much to Iacocca's dismay, this was entirely absent from Chrysler's helter-skelter scheme of things. "I simply had no idea that I wouldn't be able to get hold of the right numbers so that we could begin to attack some of Chrysler's basic problems," Iacocca says.

Trying to explain how a perceptive "bean counter" like Townsend could have been so lax, at least in Iacocca's framework, the Chrysler chairman contends that Townsend was so concerned with the next quarter's profits that he let long-range planning take a subordinate role. As the result of Townsend's downgrading of engineering, once Chrysler's ace of aces, according to Iacocca, Chrysler lost its chance to set the industry pace in new-car and -truck development. Share-holders did not object, because Townsend did produce a number of good profits and good dividend years, even if he did so at the expense of long-term company and dealership health. Moreover, the Chrysler board was uninformed about the true state of company finances and let Townsend run his own show—a throwback to the cavalier days of Walter Chrysler and K. T. Keller.

It was bad enough that Townsend had no long-term overview, Iacocca says. But Townsend, who gave up the chairmanship in 1976 with the boast that his term had "put $10 million into my pocket," was guilty of a cardinal sin for car men: he "really didn't like the car business," according to Iacocca, who fathered the Mustang.

For years in the early 1970s, after Chevrolet's Vega and Ford's Pinto had invaded the subcompact market against the Volkswagen Beetle and Rabbit and the rising influx of economy cars from Japan, Townsend vetoed proposals from Chrysler engineering for a competitive subcompact. He told one quarterly news conference after another that the economy-car market, below that of Chrysler's domestic Aspen and Volare compacts, never would amount to much.

Iacocca's observation that Townsend really was turned off by the guts of the car business was confirmed in another way: his absence from press and dealer previews, from factory events, and from labor negotiating sessions. Not even Walter Chrysler, K.

T. Keller, or Tex Colbert had been so aloof—and the Townsend era at Chrysler tells a great deal about the value of having "hands-on" officers in key positions over "figure filbert" money men unaccustomed to developing or manufacturing a product.

Yet it must be recognized that Townsend delivered the goods for scandal-plagued Chrysler in more years than he didn't. If he was no jazzy introducer of a youth-oriented Mustang or flip communicator with a gift for the headline remark, Townsend *had* mastered the science (in some slow seasons the art) of building cars and selling them to the factory's major customers, the dealers. "I've never built a car that wasn't sold," said the cocky native of Flint, who had been born in the GM factory city on May 12, 1919. "The big thing is volume."

Townsend had majored in accounting at the University of Michigan and finished second in his class in graduate business school at Ann Arbor, with a professor recalling that he had "never taught a student who had a greater flair for accounting and financial analysis." After serving in the Navy during World War II, Townsend joined the newly-formed Detroit accounting firm of Touche, Ross, Bailey and Smart—among whose clients was Chrysler. Townsend began to conduct the yearly Chrysler audit in 1947 and ten years later landed at Chrysler as comptroller. Only thirty-eight when he joined Chrysler,

Townsend was "on a roll," as a thirty-three-year-old whiz named Iacocca was at Ford.

Under orders from Colbert to improve profitability, Townsend installed three basic programs that had been used for years before at GM and Ford: A current-profit system to monitor costs on a daily basis; a capital investment program to control outlays for tools and machinery; and a forward cost-control program on coming new vehicles. Townsend's budgeteers were feared throughout the company, and old-timers were shocked when the youthful executive predicted he would be Chrysler president in two years.

As the ambitious power to be reckoned with, Townsend roamed the Chrysler network as Iacocca did twenty years later. He bought computers here, cut redundant operations there, and generally favored conservative GM-like styling. After he rose to administrative vice-president in December 1960, he ordered the immediate ouster of some seven thousand white-collar employees, about 15 percent of the total salaried workforce. This "bloodbath," as many called it, saved the corporation $50 million a year but lopped off more than a few seniority hands with weeks or months to go before pension vesting. It was cruel, but it took the public's mind off the Newberg episode and won Townsend the presidency on July 21, 1961. The corruption-free Townsend was widely regarded as Chrysler's hope for survival.

Ever sure of himself, unlike the fickle Colbert who more often than not acted according to the advice of the last person with whom he had discussed a problem, Townsend merged the Chrysler-Imperial and Plymouth divisions; ordered the high-priced DeSoto discarded; closed an Imperial assembly plant in Detroit; and hired the sales vice-president of American Motors, Virgil Boyd, who had led the successful Rambler marketing campaign there, to head up Chrysler's sales. Townsend scrapped another longstanding Chrysler taboo and formed a financial loan subsidiary, Chrysler Financial, just as GM and Ford had done. And he raided Ford for a new styling vice-president.

It all had a strong resemblance to the surgery performed on the Chrysler carcass two decades later by Iacocca, who also wielded a sharp knife. The New York financial writers honored Townsend as the club's man of the year. *Time* magazine, calling Chrysler "the comeback story of U.S. business," awarded Townsend a cover portrait—fully two years before *Time* and *Newsweek* were to similarly toast Iacocca in the same week's issue over the success of the Mustang.

Among many innovations brought to Chrysler at this time were the pentastar logo, still in use; the five-year, 50,000-mile powertrain warranty, emulated by all competitors for five years, then discontinued for cost reasons when U.S. new-car quality slumped in the late 1960s; new assembly plants outside the Detroit area; and a division for establishing factory-owned dealerships that initially was successful but later was to become an albatross despised by independently owned dealers charging unequal competition.

Townsend's moves bore bountiful fruit. Profits, always the name of the game for a "bean counter" like Townsend, soared from $9 million in 1961 to $239.5 million in 1965. Market share rose to an eight-year high of 15 percent. In July 1967, a year when profits would reach $203 million, Love stepped down as chairman and Townsend succeeded him, with "dealer man" Virgil Boyd elevated to president.

But then what the master accountant had built slowly began to unravel. The descending cycle probably was rooted in 1964, when Townsend caved in to a UAW strike after only a week and agreed to literally all the major demands made by then—UAW President Walter P. Reuther and the new director of the union's Chrysler department, the astute Douglas A. Fraser. Reuther and Fraser, union-first men who sensed that the last thing Townsend wanted was another hundred-day strike, won the biggest gains in UAW history for a single contract showdown.

Chrysler's "surrender" package, inevitably matched by an astonished GM and Ford, set a high-labor-cost precedent that fifteen years later was to open the floodgates wide for cheaper-to-build small cars from Japan. Ironically, it was Fraser, appointed by Iacocca to the Chrysler board in 1980, who was credited for keeping Chrysler workers in tune with Iacocca's rebuilding efforts through the bleak bail-out years.

Whether an Iacocca in command of Chrysler during 1964 would have folded so abjectly to UAW demands is not easy to answer. The Big Three have taken turns setting an industrywide pattern every three years, often after the "point" company has endured a nationwide strike. Obviously, Iacocca is no labor-baiter, as Walter Chrysler and K. T. Keller were. On the other hand, he drove a hard bargain with the UAW when Chrysler needed sizable concessions from the workers in 1982, and flatly refused to reopen the contract a year early, in the fall of 1984, after the UAW regained many concessions in contract renewal talks with GM and Ford. Chrysler workers cheer Iacocca when he tours the plants—a token of affection that no other top auto executive had received in the past.

Townsend, having reached his goal of a Chrysler recovery, started to pursue other interests from his chairman's office. The reins he had held over product development staffs loosened noticeably in the late 1960s, and the large boxy models, which had not been seen since the 1950s, emerged just as market tastes were shifting to smaller cars. The 1969 models, including enlarged and heavier Chrysler New Yorkers and Plymouth Furys, hit a stone-cold market, and sales plummeted.

Unruffled as usual, though some insiders thought he was growing bored with the job, Townsend approached the latest Chrysler crisis with his usual faith that the daily "numbers" would pull the company through again. No other top auto executive in recent years has relied as religiously as Townsend on day-by-day reports of sheer statistics—the previous day's production, accumulated shipments for the month, scheduled volume, cash on hand, retail sales, new orders, and finally a comparison of sales, production, and orders.

As Iacocca later said of Townsend, his emphasis on the short-term neglected the long haul. After all, accountants instinctively are geared to the moment's cash flow and tax liabilities, and while a finance man like GM Chairman Roger Smith has shown a remarkable adaptability to change and growth, such flexibility proved to be foreign to Townsend's nature. Besides, he had nurtured his forty-five-year-old accountant pal from Touche, Ross as his back-up executive and heir apparent—John J. Riccardo.

Riccardo, who had joined Chrysler in 1959 and risen through the ranks, was heading up Dodge division when he was named to replace Virgil Boyd as president in January 1970 after the 1969 product disaster. Riccardo looked forward to a twenty-year run as president and then chairman of Chrysler; Townsend promised to leave "well before my sixty-fifth birthday." Riccardo never challenged Townsend's authority seriously, even as troubles mushroomed. Eight years later, it was a shaken Chairman John Riccardo who secretly met former Ford president Lee Iacocca and implored him to rescue the sinking ship.

6

OPERATION SURVIVAL
BEGINS

S O CALAMITOUS HAD BEEN PUBLIC RECEPTION to Chrysler's enlarged 1969 models that corporate profits tumbled to $99 million that year, from $302.9 million in 1968. Townsend laid off 11,300 of Chrysler's 140,000 workers and, as sales kept plummeting, ordered three budget retrenchments in one year while demanding a total revamping of Chrysler's 1969 models, which had not been planned until 1971 on the 1972 models.

Townsend's reputation as a financial genius was on the line—and he would go to any length to protect it. He insisted on maintaining the stock dividend at two dollars a share, the same as Chrysler had paid out in the three profitable years from 1966 through 1968. (The dividend would be one of the first sacrifices under Iacocca's regime, symbolizing as it did throughout Chrysler's history a corporate philosophy that divided the "owners" of the business from the workers who built the products and the customers who bought them.)

Nicknamed "the flamethrower" by subordinates because of his short-fused outbursts when crisis situations erupted, as they frequently did in those days, Riccardo was far more of a brooder by nature than Townsend. He delved into problems, often agonizing over solutions, whereas Townsend turned to his ever-present numbers and imperiously handed down instant fixes and remedies. However, Riccardo was not as wedded to past product codes and was more inclined to match his competitors' moves and banish such long-standing Chrysler no-nos as small subcompact cars, four-cylinder engines, and front-wheel drive.

A devout Roman Catholic who attended morning mass almost daily, Riccardo must have resorted to prayer frequently to help untangle Chrysler from the recurring traumas of the 1970s. Riccardo's first year as president, 1970, brought a $7.6 million loss, the company's first since 1959. Townsend reluctantly cut the dividend to sixty cents a share.

A prominent casualty of Townsend's elevation of Riccardo to the presidency was Robert Anderson, a Chrysler executive vice-president whom many in Detroit regarded as the best product man in Chrysler's stable. Anderson, now chairman or Rockwell International, might have saved the company from a number of the product deficiencies that plagued it through the 1970s, had he, instead of Riccardo, risen to the presidency.

Anderson had found it difficult to work for Townsend in the late 1960s, however, just as Riccardo did in the early 1970s. "[Townsend] turned into a different guy," Anderson recalls. "His outlook, his approach, his ability to take counsel and advice changed. He became short-tempered, a little heavy on the martinis from time to time and unfeeling about people and the things he would say to them in front of groups. I don't know what brought it about, but he almost changed personalities."

A financial officer at Chrysler who admired Townsend's ability as a decisive administrator but sensed that he was often acting irrationally came to the conclusion that no chief executive officer of an automaker should serve more than ten years. Even Iacocca, a moderate drinker with high marks for circumspect behavior toward associates and underlings, has spoken of the rigors of serving too long in the same top-level job.

Adding to the pressure on the new president in 1970 was the introduction by Chevrolet of the subcompact Vega, with an all-aluminum engine; it was matched by Ford's Pinto. Chrysler had steered clear of the subcompact field, costing its hard-pressed dealers a crack at the small-car market. Results at the box office grew worse through 1970 and, in a foretaste of what would be almost a death blow ten years later, lenders tightened the clamps on Chrysler in the wake of the midyear bankruptcy of the giant Penn Central Transportation Company.

The shock of Penn Central's bankruptcy filing in June 1970 spilled over with lightning speed onto Chrysler, already wounded by a sales downturn. Banks found Chrysler Financial in a state of grave vulnerability because of insufficient reserves to meet commercial-paper obligations.

Fearing an involuntary-bankruptcy action that could throttle Chrysler sales and force a big selloff by shareholders, Townsend and Riccardo enlisted the aid of the chairman of Chrysler's lead bank who, with help from the Federal Reserve Bank and after nonstop SOS pleas to bankers by Chrysler's senior executives, managed to win sufficient funding for Chrysler Financial to weather the storm.

The 1970 experience gave the new president a rough christening and touched off a continuous round of world-wide visitations to banks that was not to end until Riccardo retired as chairman in September 1979, with Chrysler in the midst of desperate negotiations to save itself through federal loan guarantees. When Iacocca joined Chrysler, he couldn't get over the fact that Riccardo had spent so much time courting bankers instead of architecting new products or devising programs to open untapped markets that the company could enter.

It's worth noting, however, that Riccardo was a "bean counter" like his mentor Townsend. His solution to sales slumps, once the banks had been cajoled into ponying up $330 million in fresh money, was to tighten the personnel ranks. Some six thousand white-collar workers were laid off.

Once again, Chrysler managed to recover from a crisis as the whole auto market regained strength. Chrysler's restyled 1971-model intermediate cars paced a company comeback that continued until 1974. Townsend and Riccardo matched the new domestic subcompact cars from GM and Ford, as well as the rising tide of small cars from Japan, with the purchase of a 15 percent interest in Mitsubishi; Chrysler could now import subcompacts: the Dodge Colt and the Plymouth Cricket.

The decision not to tool up for a domestic subcompact car was rooted in lean finances as much as in a chairman's fondness for bigger cars. Spending in 1971 was the lowest for any year since 1963, although the company was selling 1.1 million more vehicles. "We were using borrowed money to pay dividends and interest, instead of spending for new models," an outside director on the Chrysler board recalled. "It was a holding operation."

It was an operation riding for another fall. In the spring of 1973, GM's executive committee, seemingly with prophetic powers, decided to downsize every car line over the next five years. That October, just as Chrysler was introducing a redesigned line of full-sized cars, Israel went to war with Egypt, Jordan, and Syria. The Yom Kippur conflict prompted the Organization of Petroleum Exporting Countries (OPEC) to boycott shipments of oil to Israel's biggest supporter, the United States. It was a nightmare for the entire U.S. industry, but Chrysler took the toughest beating for lack of suddenly-popular domestic subcompact cars.

With lengthy lines at gas stations and big "gas guzzler" cars as popular as furnaces on the equator, Chrysler plunged back into the red, losing $52 million in 1974. Townsend, now eager to leave the battered vessel, ordered a tried-and-true formula: Nearly one-third of the workforce was chopped between 1974 and 1975, including 80 percent of the engineers, many working on future products. With sales sinking, more debt was sold. The doom-and-gloom syndrome was bedeviling Chrysler again.

Then, as the oil embargo ended and Chrysler sought to recoup from the early 1974 disaster, Townsend made a last typical move that, in retrospect, could be viewed as a model of self-destruction. He ordered sharp increases in the production of 1975 models. But a recession was getting underway, and the overproduced cars began piling up for lack of dealer orders.

Aggravating the inventory run-up was the sorry quality of most Chrysler cars, which had never really been upgraded since the late 1960s. "We were building and shipping junk," a Chrysler production executive remembered.

Chrysler went into a massive survival scheme that included omitting dividends for the first time since 1933. Said an irate shareholder, "You don't go to a doctor to have a will drawn up. You don't go to an accountant to build a car."

With the market share continuing to tumble in 1975 (it finished below 12 percent) and a record full-year loss of $259.5 million shaping up, Townsend decided to pack it in. He announced in July 1976, that he would step down as chairman the following October 1 and recommended that John Riccardo be elevated to chairman, and that the vice-president for North American operations, Eugene Cafiero, a New York-born industrial engineer who had joined the company in 1953, be promoted to president.

The Chrysler board dutifully followed Townsend's succession suggestion in 1976, despite concerns among several outside directors over Riccardo's reputation for feistiness and over the retention of an accountant in the number-one position. On the latter point, Townsend had a typically brusque defense that would be antithetical to the inclinations of an Iacocca or of a Don Petersen at Ford: "At this level of management, it doesn't make a difference what your background is. We don't design or build cars at this level. We set the objectives and policies and monitor the progress."

Meeting the press in a crowded conference room on the ground floor of the Chrysler headquarters building, Chairman Riccardo and President Cafiero surprised students of the auto business by disagreeing on the future road each thought the ailing company should travel. Said Riccardo: Chrysler would compete "in all new segments of the market as they develop," signifying for the first time Chrysler's plan to produce domestic subcompact cars. Said Cafiero: Chrysler would select segments so as to develop new cars from fewer platforms. Riccardo, realizing what his president was saying, abruptly cut him off and fielded another question. It was a bleak omen.

The difference in philosophies between the two men widened in the three years before Iacocca came to Chrysler, 1975-1978. It was Cafiero's product concept, centering on limited platforms and segment eclectisism, that prevailed under the Chrysler of Iacocca, ironically. Riccardo, a throwback to the full-line approach of Keller, Colbert, and Townsend, was to fail in his comeback efforts. Yet it had become such a fast track at Chrysler, which lacked the many experienced managers of GM and Ford, that Riccardo gained the chairmanship after only sixteen years with the company. Such a career climax would have taken at least thirty years at GM or Ford.

Riccardo came to office with the company in a bottomless whirlpool. Lifesavers were needed fast, and Riccardo set to work with typical determination. His own reputation was on the line, and he knew that speed was of the essence if Chrysler were to survive and if he were to serve as chairman into the 1980s. He was gone before 1980, but not for lack of trying.

7

"WHO CAN
I TURN TO?"

THE JOHN RICCARDO WHO CLIMBED TO THE top rung of Chrysler in 1975 was besieged from all sides. Orderly succession had been unknown throughout Chrysler's post–World War II history, but no previous chief executive officer had faced the problems that stared the brooding Riccardo in the face: New-car and -truck inventories had mushroomed to nearly 400,000 units, costing the already-strapped company about $1.5 million each working day. The cutbacks imposed by Townsend had angered the UAW, which made no secret of its plan to name Chrysler the Big Three target for 1976 contract negotiations. The federal government was passing one auto regulation after another, spurred on by the 1974 oil embargo.

Worst of all, Chrysler had delayed sorely needed new-car development programs because of the cash crunch. Without a massive infusion of funds, catching up to GM's front-wheel-drive changeovers would be next to impossible. Moreover, the launch of the Plymouth Volare and Dodge Aspen compacts in the fall of 1974 had been marred by inadequate road testing, forcing engine stallouts and hood latch defects, which prompted a recall of 3.5 million cars for free dealer repairs at a cost to the factory of more than $200 million.

President Cafiero, Chrysler's first chief operating officer in twenty years to boast a manufacturing background, concentrated on cleaning up this disaster and on speeding up future new products. But not even the technical-minded Cafiero could stanch the tidal wave of Aspen and Volare recalls, which set a Chrysler record.

Early on in his presidency Cafiero parted company with Riccardo on basic issues to the extent that they remained barely on speaking terms. Cafiero could not salvage enough funds from the Riccardo-ordered cutbacks to bring in the front-wheel-drive Omni and Horizon subcompacts in time for launch in the fall of 1977. The first front-wheel-drive subcompacts from any of the Big Three members arrived in January 1978, which had been considered until then a terrible time to introduce any new models. That Omni and Horizon made it all was a near-miracle.

Meanwhile, Riccardo was devoting an inordinate amount of time to courting the company's forty main banks, visiting each no fewer than three times between 1976 and 1979. Why he felt this to be so necessary can be explained better by his personality than by Chrysler's financial performance after he assumed the chairmanship. The sales upturn that followed the end of the oil embargo lifted Chrysler's profits to $422.6 million in 1976, despite the Aspen and Volare launch fiasco, and to $163.2 million in 1977. Yet unlike Townsend, Riccardo steered the vessel as if it were the Titanic approaching hidden icebergs. Once burned, twice shy, and Riccardo could always see troubles on the horizon.

At the same time, Riccardo tracked the often-unrealistic Townsend in acceding to union demands. A 1976 contract settlement with the UAW, again too expensive for Chrysler in a desperate attempt to avoid a lengthy strike, boosted the critical production break-even cost by about a hundred dollars a car. And showing his kinship with his forebears, Riccardo rejected a UAW demand that a union representative be seated on the company board.

Riccardo also made a blunder in terms of governmental and public relations—one that deepened the company's image gap. As the industry's point man, he challenged almost singlehandedly the mushrooming crescendo of regulations emanating from Congress and the Department of Transportation appointees of the new Democratic President, Jimmy Carter. The safety and emissions devices imposed on the auto industry wound up costing about $750 a car, no small sum to cash-strained Chrysler, and Riccardo lashed out at the feds and their "intrusion" into the private sector. He ended up retreating from an impossible antiregulatory campaign ("don't fight city hall"), a campaign he might not have seen fit to stage at all had he anticipated how difficult the retreat might have made Chrysler's drive for federal loan guarantees a few years down the road.

Could Riccardo and Cafiero do nothing right? Their batting average was a hard-won .200–.250 at best. But it was bolstered by one of the few home runs the Italian-American duo was to deliver for the Chrysler aggregation. This was the hiring in late 1976 of savvy car development engineer Harold Sperlich, then forty-seven, who had been peremptorily fired by Henry Ford II a month earlier for abrasively pushing small-car reforms, which chairman of Ford found repugnant.

Sperlich had been Lee Iacocca's favorite product-planning technician. He had been instrumental in Americanizing the Spanish-built Fiesta minicompact as an import for Ford, but neither he nor the falling-from-favor Iacocca could sell the boss on a domestic subcompact program aimed at meeting the oncoming competition from the Chrysler Omni and Horizon and the GM X-cars. Iacocca and Sperlich secretly worked out a powertrain purchase deal with Japan's esteemed small-car builder Soichiro Honda, only to have Henry II exclaim, "No Japanese product is going under the hood with my name on it!"

Iacocca was stunned in mid-1976 when Ford demanded that Iacocca fire Sperlich for "personal reasons." He refused to axe his loyal product executive personally and assigned the chore to executive vice-president William O. Bourke. Sperlich never did learn why Ford landed on him so crudely, and could only have been pleased when Bourke himself was dumped by Ford in the spring of 1980 after the absence of small front-wheel-drive cars at Ford resulted in a sales and profits bath.

The fact that Sperlich quickly signed on at Chrysler set the stage in a way for the coming of Iacocca and several dozen other Ford executives a few years later. Machiavellian historians have called the Ford-to-Chrysler shift of Sperlich, now Chrysler's president, a well-planned "plot" by Iacocca, who knew he would be pursuing the same course and wanted Sperlich in place at Chrysler first. The scenario would be accurate, however, only if one could predict all the winners of the next day's horse races. Why would Cafiero even bring in the rejected Sperlich, who might be an Iacocca "mole" only there to undercut Cafiero himself?

In any event, Sperlich brought to Chrysler expertise on small cars and a determination to upgrade the company's lagging products. His prime early focus at Chrysler was the K-body compact car, due in 1980.

However, increasingly burdensome tooling expenditures for subcompacts and full-size cars, combined with a general auto sales dip, brought red ink back to Chrysler in 1978 to the tune of $204.6 million. The 1978 reversal repeated an old refrain: Blame-the-boss and get-a-new-one had been a game played at Chrysler since Colbert dethroned Keller, Townsend displaced Colbert, and Riccardo himself upended Townsend.

The same game had been practiced at Ford, and Iacocca had seen one president after another give way to the whims of the entrenched chairman, Henry Ford II; Iacocca himself was superseded by the rising Philip Caldwell. After all, the losing Detroit Tigers and Detroit Lions, professional baseball and football teams, were undergoing frequent managerial changes, so why not the automakers who were the Motor City area's principal employers?

Continuity, as pursued in the top management ranks at GM, was given lip service at Chrysler and Ford, but lip service only. Iacocca had seen them come and go at Ford; many were his personal hires and fires, and he was to sack thirty of thirty-three vice-presidents at Chrysler. His rationale was to purge "deadwood" wedded to old ways of doing things, plus a deep-seated conviction that "creative tension" was needed lest a company revert to stagnation after a fresh upturn period.

In Riccardo's case, as much as he had accomplished in trimming Chrysler down, he knew that without a drastically overhauled product development and manufacturing capability Chrysler was finished. It was only a matter of time. Cafiero had failed to accomplish the sought-after reform and would take the first rap, but Riccardo knew instinctively that the house-cleaning would reach the chairman's seat as well. Besides, he had developed a heart condition, which brought a personal medical concern into the picture, although few knew about it.

Where would Riccardo have turned in 1978 had Iacocca hung on at Ford, without receiving the royal pink slip from King Henry II? Former GM group vice-president John Z. DeLorean was free, and not yet disgraced. A headhunter quietly called by Riccardo was prepared to go after a pair of GM hotshots, reportedly Robert Stempel and Lloyd Reuss, but feelers in their direction got lukewarm responses at best in the turmoil of 1978. (Reuss and Stempel now head GM's two main car operations groups and are on track for the GM presidency in 1987.)

Had Iacocca been unavailable, Riccardo most likely would have turned to another insider for advancement to the presidency. There would have been no one in command with the charisma to wangle $1.2 billion in loan guarantees from Washington, much less to persuade enough Americans that the new K-cars or E-cars to follow were worth buying at the constantly inflated prices of the early 1980s. Luck had played its part in making possible a move that worked to everyone's advantage.

8

OUTWARD

BOUND

I
T WAS 1975, THE FIRST YEAR AFTER THE WATER-
gate revelations had forced the U.S. President
to resign. The auto industry was emerging
from the oil-embargo shock wave. And the all-
powerful chairman of the nation's second-largest
automaker suddenly began an investigation into the
private activities of the company's president and his
own heir apparent, Lee Iacocca.

The investigation, which involved the designa-
tion of a former Michigan Supreme Court justice
as a "special prosecutor," à la Watergate, cost Ford
nearly $2 million. Iacocca, until then a Ford loyalist
to the core, has since declared that he should have
quit in 1975. He was exonerated of all suspicion of

payola from Ford's travel and sales-promotion agency. He now believes that Henry Ford II was hopeful that he would resign, innocent or not. The way was being paved for the chairman to lower the boom on Iacocca in 1978.

Why didn't Iacocca pull out, then? For one thing, he was a Ford thoroughbred, unable to sever the cord from a company that was paying him close to $1 million a year in salary and bonuses. And though he won't admit to his political finesse now, he was convinced that in a showdown between Henry Ford II and himself, enough outside directors would side with Iacocca to save him and possibly even force a shift in the chairmanship.

Lesson in management: Money and power still talk, no matter how many outside directors like your work and your personality. Iacocca, usually a perceptive judge of personnel and a quick antagonist of anyone who blunders, in this case misread the dynamics of Ford Motor Company's control tower when the chips finally came down. He had observed that Bunkie Knudsen's resignation as Ford president in 1969 after only a year in office resulted from Knudsen's lack of support among board members. But who actually counted was Henry II, board or no board.

Greed, Iacocca has said, is the deadliest sin of all when it serves to keep in place executives who refuse to heed signals to go. He doesn't add that many linger on who have nowhere to go, including Iacocca himself in 1976. That was the same year Riccardo replaced Townsend as chairman of Chrysler, a realignment that had been urged by the retiring Townsend, who clearly would never have recruited Iacocca from Ford. Iacocca had too independent a personality to suit someone like Townsend, who contended that all Chrysler needed was a clone of himself from inside the company.

Henry Ford II did not call off the hound dogs where Iacocca was concerned. In 1976, not only did the monarchial chairman order the discharge of Harold Sperlich, whom Iacocca had favored as the next head of Ford's North American auto operations, but also of a particularly close pal of Iacocca's William Winn, who had staged dealer shows and special productions for Ford. The double-ouster blow, hard enough as it was for Iacocca to stomach, did not remotely come close to the shocker handed out by Henry Ford II in 1977.

McKinsey & Company, a management consultant firm, was installed by Henry Ford II to reorganize the top echelons at Ford. McKinsey's main conclusion was put into effect in April 1977: the establishment of a three-man "office of the executive" in place of the standard chairman-and-president system.

To Iacocca's chagrin, Philip Caldwell was named vice-chairman and number-two executive in the Ford top management structure. Iacocca regarded the upgrading of Caldwell, a stolid corporate type

who once had reported to him, as a "public humil-
iation, like the guy in the stockade in the center of
town." Yet he refused to resign, declaring that he
would not "crawl out of there with my tail between
my legs."

In June 1978, Henry's younger brother, William
Clay Ford, was added to the "office of chief executive," and Caldwell was appointed deputy chief
executive officer. The handwriting was not only on
the wall, but on Iacocca's forehead. Henry II,
according to Iacocca, had turned so cold he would
not even give his long-time president a decent
explanation of the top-level restructuring.

In Ford's defense, he has told his own biographer
that ample reasons existed for lowering the boom
on Iacocca, whom he had hoped would take the
hints and resign. Ford's biography will not be published until after his death, however, leaving the
world with only Iacocca's version of what took place
in June and July 1978.

Outside directors were informed of June 12 that
the chairman wanted to expel the out-of-favor president. Iacocca fans on the board reportedly resisted
the powerful chairman, and several even met with
Iacocca privately to explore ways for healing the
breach. The coup de grâce fell on the night of July
12, when Henry II overrode the reluctance of outside board members, declared "it's him or me," and
announced that Iacocca would be officially "asked
to resign" the next day.

That night, *Automotive News* publisher Keith Crain called Iacocca at home to ask him if the rumors were true. Iacocca surmises that Henry II had asked his son Edsel to tip off the publisher so that "the news of my firing [would] reach me through a third party. Henry was a pro at turning the screws."

The next afternoon, Henry Ford and William Clay Ford finished the execution proceedings in a forty-five-minute meeting. Iacocca insists no specific reasons for Henry's disfavor were disclosed beyond Henry's statement that the motive was "personal." Henry, according to Iacocca, only added, "Sometimes you just don't like somebody."

It was decided that the resignation would take effect on October 15, 1978, Iacocca's fifty-fourth birthday. Iacocca had worked at Ford for thirty-two years, during which Henry II had been chairman and chief executive officer. Iacocca would move from the president's office in the "Glass House," Ford's headquarters building on Michigan Avenue in the Detroit suburb of Dearborn, to another location.

That was that, except that Iacocca had the last word. He says he told Henry: "Your timing stinks. We've just made a billion eight for the second year in a row. That's three and a half billion in the past two years. But mark my words, Henry. You may never see a billion eight again. And do you know why? Because you don't know how the fuck we made it in the first place!"

Iacocca asserts that Henry Ford "never understood" how the company really sold cars and trucks and brought in revenues and profits. This statement is a little hard to believe, the implication being that Ford was a dunce with a crown and Iacocca was a genius who served as prime minister and chancellor of the exchequer both. In any event, Iacocca was through. He took satisfaction from the fact that press kits of the restyled 1979 Mustang, the smash-hit sports car he had sired at Ford fifteen years earlier, had been mailed that very week of his demise with his own photo featured prominently.

In a somewhat naive effort to explain the circumstances of his dismissal, Iacocca asks why the outside directors who originally opposed Ford's impulsive action refused to stand up to him or resign themselves when the final blow landed. "To this day," he has stated, "I can't figure out how the board members can defend their decision, to themselves or to anyone else." Iacocca is indirectly pointing a finger at the bottom-line impotence of the corporate board of directors systems. The chairman of the company almost always nominates the outside and inside members, whose election or reelection is a formality, even when the company is doing poorly. Fees to outside directors, who serve on one or two board committees, reach as much as $15,000 a year currently for up to twelve board meetings, in the case of corporate giants like GM or Ford. The outside director who is "not compatible" with the company's senior management is so rare as to be a freak, in spite of the clearly-spelled-out fiduciary duty of directors to serve the interests of *all* shareholders and not merely those of management or the big stockholders.

Back at Chrysler, although 1978 industry passenger-car sales were rebounding to a record 11.1 million units, the tires remained stuck in the mud. Chrysler's loss for the third quarter had escalated to a record $158.8 million, and Riccardo feared a financial crisis of overwhelming proportions if the 1979 model year was a flop. The sudden availability of Iacocca, whom Riccardo knew only casually, was a blessing in the open.

The media had made a banner headline story of Iacocca's firing, prompting the inevitable speculation that he had been sacked for misconduct. Companies in need of an experienced marketing and production executive ignored the rumors, and he was besieged by offers. Although he considered some from nonautomotive companies, he decided that he was a "car man" to the core. Several major auto suppliers contacted him also, yet Iacocca felt he had too much gasoline in his blood even to venture into the relatively secure area of parts production. Renault, which was negotiating to buy a controlling interest in American Motors, beat Riccardo to the punch with a proposition, but it was not seriously considered because Iacocca felt he would be subordinate to the interests of the French automaker in Paris and to the French government, which owns Renault. "I had to be in the mainstream of the car business," he recalls. "What the hell. It's like a guy telling a pianist, 'You're so good—why don't you try the saxophone?'"

Money was no problem, meaning that Iacocca could have retired with a tidy cushion. He had earned an aggregated $4.2 million in salary and bonuses from 1972 through 1977 at Ford. His severance agreement provided for $400,000 in cash, $22,500 a month for a year from October 15, 1978, retirement benefits of $178,500 a year until he reached the age of 65, and $175,000 a year thereafter. His property included a large condominium in Boca Raton, Florida, as well as the fifteen-room split-level house in posh Bloomfield Hills, the northern Detroit suburb where nearly all the top auto executives live. He could have become a consultant or a corporate raider or a dimly remembered figure out of the auto industry's past, like Townsend or Colbert or Bunkie Knudsen.

But Iacocca was not yet fifty-five. He loved the spotlight shining on those new cars every year and, coincidentally, on himself. And he, above all, wanted to prove Henry Ford II was wrong and that the man he had fired could redeem himself and teach Henry a lesson.

If this sounds like revenge, it is. The vehicle for Iacocca's revenge would be Chrysler, for there was nowhere else that the quintessential "car guy" could turn. The timing couldn't have been better for either Chrysler or Iacocca, in truth, since a smoother operation across town in Highland Park would have left Iacocca unsummoned.

The only call Iacocca needed did come, somewhat to his surprise. Henry Ford II might have listened to those outside directors if he had had any idea where Iacocca was heading!

9

CHRYSLER: FROM CRISIS
TO CRUSADER

T TOOK LEE IACOCCA TWO MONTHS IN THE SUM-
mer and early fall of 1978 to decide that there
was a Chrysler in his future, after all. Not since
Walter Chrysler himself came out of retirement
in 1924 (the year Iacocca was born) to reorganize
the precursor company of Chrysler had such an
automotive luminary agreed to take charge of a
sinking automaker.

In fact, Iacocca insists today that he never would
have succumbed to the pleas of the desperate John
Riccardo had he known what lay ahead for him.
Iacocca infers that he might not have taken on the
Chrysler challenge were it not for the "go for it"
assent of his ailing wife, Mary, who was deeply

wounded by the way Ford had dumped Lee; she even suggested he write a book about the experience!

The role of outside directors in nailing down another crisis-born management change was repeated at Chrysler in 1978. Just as George Love had stepped in to take over the chairmanship from Tex Colbert in the early 1960s, Riccardo got direct aid in meeting with Iacocca from both J. Richardson Dilworth, an outside director who represented the Rockerfeller interests, and Wall Street attorney Louis Warren.

It isn't clear whether Richardson, Warren, and other non-management directors prodded Riccardo, or vice versa. Riccardo said later, "I picked Lee for the company. It was my suggestion that we hire him." In any event, all concerned made it clear that bagging Iacocca was priority one, and Riccardo received an unreserved green light from the board. The urgency was intensified after Riccardo's initial phone-calls to several up-and-coming GM executives, whom he knew personally better than he knew Iacocca, were not even returned.

What Riccardo might have done to find a successor had Iacocca rebuffed Chrysler has never been even speculated upon by Chrysler directors or Riccardo himself. Since the negotiations between Iacocca and Riccardo were conducted in utmost secrecy, it's even possible, though highly doubtful, that the outside world never might have learned of the Riccardo-Iacocca talks in the event of a firm "thanks, but no thanks" on the part of the ousted Ford president.

Iacocca, without waiting for a come-aboard phone call from Riccardo, charted a grandiose international automotive scenario involving himself and his old Ford pal (now at Chrysler) Hal Sperlich. It was more than the makework daydream of a suddenly out-to-pasture executive. The project as first envisioned by Iacocca and several other imaginative executives in the late 1970s (including then-American Motors Chairman Gerald Meyers and John DeLorean) was the only path to survival for small U.S. automakers against the giants—GM, Ford, the Germans as a unit, "Japan, Inc.," and possibly Renault-Peugeot from France.

Iacocca called the proposed new conglomerate "Global Motors." Under its umbrella would fall Chrysler and American Motors from the United States, Volkswagen from West Germany, and possibly Fiat from Italy. Chrysler would have brought to the confederation its ties with Mitsubishi of Japan and with Peugeot of France. It seemed a natural alliance to ward off the almighty automakers in the United States, as well as the "Japan, Inc." consortium that operated with total immunity from the impact of American-type antitrust laws.

Indeed, antitrust policies in Washington proved to be the stumbling block to any hopes for turning Global Motors from a pipedream into reality. The

Department of Justice and the Federal Trade Commission, under both Republican and Democratic Administrations, had since the 1950s effectively barred linkages of U.S. automakers amongst themselves. For the "Little Three"—Chrysler, AMC, and VW of America—to pool resources would have been a "federal case" for sure, Iacocca was advised. The domestic automakers could not even exchange data on meeting federal safety and emissions standards, lest they be accused of antitrust violations.

It wasn't until the election of Ronald Reagan as President in 1980 that antitrust reins were loosened to the extent of permitting many of the recent moves by no less than the number-one automaker itself. GM acquired Electronic Data Systems for $2.5 billion and joined forces with Toyota, Japan's largest auto producer, to build the Chevrolet Nova in the United States. Antitrust experts say that either move would have been forbidden under the strict-interpretation philosophy of the Justice Departments of Presidents Carter, Ford, Nixon, and Johnson.

Iacocca, once he had turned Chrysler around, revived the Global Motors concept with an approach to Ford for a merger in 1982. He also contacted VW in West Germany. Both companies rebuffed him then, and he has dropped active pursuit of the trans-ocean idea, which probably will be reborn nonetheless during the next automotive recession. Whether Iacocca himself—or an Iacocca-type go-getter—will be available to finalize Global Motors remains to be seen, however.

By October 1978, Iacocca and Riccardo were meeting frequently in and around the Detroit area. New York's Solomon Brothers investment banking firm drew up for Iacocca a list of questions to ask Riccardo, centered mostly on where Chrysler was going to obtain funds for the billion-dollar K-body replacement cars for the lagging Aspen and Volare compacts.

The inquisition was typical of Iacocca's executive style at the quarterly reviews he used so much at Ford (and subsequently took with him to Chrysler): fire was at the "witness" or "deponent" like a prosecutor, keeping him sharp and on the defensive.

Riccardo wasn't used to this tactic. But he had no choice if he wanted Iacocca to sign up. In a burst of optimism rare for the normally dour Chrysler chairman, Riccardo told Iacocca that Chrysler was sure of a quick return to profitability because of the redesigned full-size R-body cars—the Chrysler New Yorker and Dodge St. Regis—which were just reaching the market. Riccardo voiced the hope that Iacocca, the auto industry's supersalesman, could pump up enthusiasm for the high-profit R-cars as soon as he formally accepted the Chrysler presidency.

Iacocca questioned how much cash could be generated from the already-delayed R-cars to fund the top-priority K-body compacts two years away. But ever the enthusiast when a new product was there to be peddled, he was not about to turn the job offer down over such doubts, determined as he was to redeem his reputation in an automotive atmosphere. He told Riccardo that he would join Chrysler as president, with Cafiero moving to vice-chairman, if the compensation package he would forfeit at Ford were replaced.

Iacocca joined Chrysler as president and chief operating officer for a salary of $360,000 a year, the same as he had been paid at Ford (the deal required that Chairman Riccardo be raised $20,000 a year from his $340,000 salary for "matching" purposes). In addition, Chrysler would pay Iacocca $1.5 million in installments between January 2, 1979, and June 30, 1980, to replace a forfeited severance settlement from Ford and would give him an option to buy 400,000 shares of Chrysler stock. Iacocca kept his Ford pension and more than $3 million in Ford stock.

More significantly, Riccardo agreed in writing to recommend that the Chrysler board name Iacocca chief executive officer within a year. Riccardo had sought to delay this move for two years, but Iacocca said that that would be too long. The game plan called for Riccardo to stay as chairman and Cafiero, who knew nothing of the negotiations with Iacocca, as vice-chairman.

On the last Friday of October, Riccardo and a

handful of top executives finally broke the news to Cafiero. The current president was not certain what his duties as vice-chairman would be, and indeed there were none spelled out for him, so it wasn't long after Iacocca's accession in November that Cafiero pulled out completely after having tried vainly to persuade Iacocca to keep him on in a stronger management role. The "new kid on the block," however, would have none of this, realizing by this time that it was operational miscues that were the root of Chrysler's problems.

The Chrysler board met on November 2, 1978, to put its official seal of approval on the dramatic news. A news conference followed at which Iacocca made sure that national media were present. A relieved Riccardo told newsmen that Iacocca would bring more "firepower" to Chrysler.

Little did the fatigued chairman realize what lay in store for the proud Chrysler management team, most of whom had never worked anywhere else. Many of them naively believed that Iacocca would keep them in place while he ran the company, just as Bunkie Knudsen had done with Ford staff when he became Ford president in 1968, after his life-long stint at GM.

It had really happened. Lee Iacocca was captain of his own ship for the first time. The ship was leaking badly and morale among the officers and men was as shoddy as most of the cargo. But it was Iacocca's vessel to revitalize or to sink. He had no time to spare, he needed help, and he knew he had to act like a man possessed.

What did Iacocca bring to the rescue operation? His marketing intuition, which Chrysler lacked in the 1970s, was combined with a knack for conceiving vehicles at minimum cost and then building derivative models off the main base, says J. Paul Bergmoser, a retired Ford purchasing vice-president whom Iacocca persuaded to join him at Chrysler; "Lee had perhaps the best feel of the consumer and the marketplace of any top automotive executive in the business."

Capping Iacocca's skills as product developer and marketer par excellence with another quality in short supply at Chrysler. No other senior auto executive at the time could communicate internally or externally with Iacocca's flair for color and candor. No other figure from the generally bland auto industry, except Henry Ford II, could attract the attention in Detroit that he could. The Iacocca persona was, and still is, an irresistible force propelling Chrysler. He dominates meetings, even when he is merely an attender, much like a movie star or baseball hero. He dresses conservatively, but his mind span covers a wider range of interests than that of most industrial executives, and he is tuned in to the day-to-day headlines and media events that many others in the industry ignore or fluff off in their parochial concern with the day's meetings.

In 1978–79 the question that Wall Street and

many old Iacocca associates at Ford asked was whether he was over-rated. Could Iacocca really function as a successful chief executive officer and turn Chrysler around in the process? Or was he a genius of the General Patton order, superb at driving the intimidated rank-and-file troops toward fixed objectives, but unable to function as supreme commander like Eisenhower or Marshall?

There were a surprising number of skeptics as to Iacocca's ultimate leadership potential in a situation like the one Chrysler confronted. He was highly praised as a product developer and launcher—still a beneficiary of the harvests of the now fifteen-year-old Mustang—but drew low marks for financial controls and adaptability to crunches of the recurring Chrysler variety.

Competitors and former Ford employees, many of whom had felt the Iacocca lash or simply been outpointed in the marketplace by the tough-talking executive, doubted his ability to function as a "smooth" chairman of the board even while recognizing his qualifications to be a chief operating officer. Working with outside directors and bankers was not Iacocca's "thing," warned these cynics, who believed that Chrysler needed another George Love or Lynn Townsend to oversee Iacocca's operations activities.

For his part, the dispirited Riccardo wasn't about to look elsewhere. He was ready to bow out and had utter confidence in Iacocca's ability to take over *and* take charge. He had made his commitment to Iacocca and there really was no choice if Chrysler stood any chance of being saved.

10

DRAFTING THE

"FORD GUYS"

"**E**VEN THOUGH I HAVE ACTIVELY AD-
dressed the major problems facing
Chrysler," John Riccardo declared on
September 18, 1979, in his letter
announcing his retirement as Chrysler chairman,
"in the minds of many I am closely associated with
the past management of a troubled company."

The phrase "troubled company" was as mild as
a spray of cologne. When Lee Iacocca, ten months
earlier, had begun daily duty as Chrysler president
and chief operating officer, the situation had been
a corporate nightmare beyond Iacocca's wildest
expectations, unlike Ford in even the deepest of
recession years. How Iacocca untangled the admin-

istrative knots and addressed the even more horrendous specter of a financial collapse tell much about his style at a top commander's post such as he had sought vainly at Ford.

The Ford and GM methods of running departments by continuously changing income-and-outgo budgets, with fixed goals by quarters and calendar years, remained foreign to Chrysler's ways of doing business in 1978. The Chrysler system wasn't exactly haphazard, but it reminded Iacocca of a small retail operation running from day to day on whatever cash was coming in and whatever bills had to be paid that day or could be postponed. With such an unsophisticated financial operation, to Iacocca it would be insanity to expect the federal government to guarantee over a billion dollars in loans for even a major company, however big an employer it might be.

Iacocca also took immediate exception to the empires and miniempires that were directed by powerful Chrysler executive vice-presidents and vice-presidents. The sales and marketing executive vice-president, R. K. Brown, served on Chrysler's board, as had all his predecessors, but he also ran the manufacturing functions, despite the fact he had devoted his entire career to the dealer side of the business.

To Iacocca, sales and manufacturing were too distinct and specialized to be governed directly by a single individual. Chrysler had almost destroyed itself a decade earlier with the dealer-loathed "sales bank," wherein cars were produced without regard for dealer orders, and here again was a meld of sales and production under a single powerful executive.

Similarly, Engineering Vice-President Richard Vining also had purchasing, a key production-related activity, under his wing for no definable reason. Iacocca believed that manufacturing and purchasing should be combined into one staff function, and this was done before long.

Riccardo, moreover, as Chrysler chairman, monitored a number of staff activities that in most companies funnel up on the organization chart to the president. These included finance, personnel, legal and public affairs, Chrysler Leasing, and Chrysler Realty. Riccardo presumably kept his direct ties to finance, as well as to the auditor and comptroller, because of his accountant's expertise in the money area, but Iacocca felt that the strain on any chairman was too great, especially for the head of a company with as many problems as Chrysler.

As it turned out, Riccardo's retirement was hastened in 1979 by a cardiac problem that caused him to be hospitalized that spring. Riccardo's physician released him with orders to retire immediately or face the possibility of a fatal heart attack. It was to become Iacocca's show sooner than anyone had anticipated, and the new leader was learning that the house needed more than a repair here and there. It needed rebuilding from A to Z.

Iacocca also set about to realign Chrysler's committees, which he found to his utter surprise consisted of a grand total of two. There was Riccardo's Operations Committee, on which President Iacocca joined Vice-Chairman Cafiero and the comptroller, the treasurer, and the group leaders of non-automotive, international, public affairs, engineering, and the all-powerful sales/manufacturing.

There also was something called the Officers' Council, comprising thirty-one executives who met every other month. And that was all. It was not what Iacocca was used to at Ford, where tighter units meeting regularly and sharing input could zero in on problems and were in general more efficient. Besides, the fact of the matter was that Chrysler's system was not working in the sense that it was continuing the tradition of the "rimless wheel," with a chairman at the center and the spokes not otherwise connected.

"This company," Iacocca said shortly after he arrived, "took twenty-five years to become decadent ... rotten to the core." What K. T. Keller and Tex Colbert had wrought, Iacocca meant to raze and reassemble. Big egos and institutionalized substructures were squarely at risk as Iacocca carved up the old turkey.

Before Thanksgiving 1978, having spent barely three weeks in the president's chair, Iacocca began to firmly plant his brand on the Chrysler carcass. Manufacturing and its related activities, primarily the crucial area of vehicle quality and reliability, were reassigned from dealer man Brown to Engineering Vice-President Vining. The latter already listed purchasing among his responsibilities, and Iacocca thought enough of him to promote him to executive vice-president for manufacturing and purchasing. Replacing Vining as group vice-president for product planning, design, and engineering, to no one's surprise, was Hal Sperlich, Iacocca's old friend from the Ford days and now virtually the only Chrysler insider trusted by the new president.

Whether Iacocca really intended to cling to Vining with Sperlich, so intimate an associate, in place, is questionable in retrospect. A number of group vice-presidents, like Frank Anderson in manufacturing and Sidney Jeffe in engineering, could see the handwriting on the walls of their offices, but they hung on anyway until Iacocca managed to assemble the team he really wanted in command positions. Iacocca simply had to make do with what Chrysler had until his own recruits could check in.

Iacocca, no newcomer to the art of finding the right man for the right slot, realized that mere reassignments of duties or vice-presidents could not save Chrysler. What Iacocca really was striving to accomplish was a reexamination of each and every Chrysler operation by knowledgeable technicians reporting directly to him. Manufacturing was divorced from sales or product development so that each could be scrutinized closely; the previous system had, perhaps intentionally, precluded such overviews. The best efforts of previous top administrators to rationalize the organization had been continuously derailed—until Iacocca came along with his overriding mandate.

In the end, Iacocca's reshuffling of the officers he had inherited proved to be unsatisfactory. It was well-nigh impossible for Chrysler-schooled veterans like Brown, Anderson, Vining, and Jeffe to blend in with the Iacocca format or timetable. Iacocca wanted results. He couldn't deal with the status quo staffwise, although several of those who were forced out said later that his temper was as much the problem as their training.

Iacocca, out of sheer despair, turned to three Ford retired executives and persuaded them to join him at Chrysler. They were Gar Laux, who had headed sales and marketing at Ford; Paul Bergmoser, Ford's long-time purchasing chief, and Hans Matthias, who had been vice-president in charge of manufacturing.

Both Matthias and Bergmoser were regarded as the toughest cookies to have toiled for Ford or anyone else around Detroit—a reputation that drew high marks from Iacocca, who could be merciless with personnel himself. Iacocca credited Matthias for singlehandedly improving Ford's quality, and he was the first of the trio to be called to perform the same task at Chrysler. Matthias had formed a manufacturing consulting firm in Detroit after he retired in 1972, and he preferred to function as an outside consultant to Vining.

Bergmoser had been a Ford purchasing staffer for thirty years, rising to purchasing vice-president before his "early retirement" to Palm Springs in 1976 at age sixty. Iacocca called upon him at first to review Chrysler's purchasing operations and the make a report—a task the California resident was told would take a few months at most.

The third corner of the Iacocca consultant triangle was filled by Laux, who in a sense had the hardest assignment of all. Laux, had been Iacocca's general sales manager at Ford division when the Mustang was introduced, rising to general manager of Lincoln-Mercury. An affable "dealer man" who had left Ford at age fifty-one in 1968 when Knudsen became Ford president, Laux had opened a Cadillac dealership in Charlotte, North Carolina, with golfing great Arnold Palmer.

At first, Laux also agreed to consult with Iacocca on the Chrysler sales operation. But like Bergmoser, he couldn't function in the role once recommendations had been made to Iacocca and implementation became the priority. Iacocca asked Laux and Bergmoser to come aboard, and they did by the spring of 1979.

What Iacocca and his "professor-emeritus troika" spotted instantly at Chrysler was, as Matthias exclaimed, "a mess we may never unravel." Iacocca came to sneer at the vaunted Chrysler system of financial controls installed by Townsend and Riccardo, declaring "they had accounting controls, auditing controls, but no financial controls to help the operating people run their business. God, if they're there, I still haven't found them."

Bergmoser, who was to become president of Chrysler after his stint in purchasing, told Iacocca that "I have a terrific accountant's report that tells me we have lost a billion dollars. What I don't have is an analysis of how the hell we lost a billion dollars."

With Matthias on board to streamline Chrysler's creaky and quality-plagued manufacturing operation, Iacocca gave Sperlich an order to concentrate on future models at whatever cost. The essential K-body compacts, due in 1980, were not to be compromised or postponed.

Matthias was given instructions from the boss to step on any toes or make any moves he deemed necessary, even as a consultant, to update Chrysler production processes. He set up a joint UAW-Chrysler "quality program," the first in the industry, ignoring the usual adversarial relationships between the company and the union that had made such teamwork impossible in the past.

More concretely, Matthias went to the plants and asked foremen to compare the workmanship of Chrysler's cars with that of a Japanese car that he would drive in. There was literally no comparison, and the foremen knew it. No one had cared before, really. It was a revelation.

In the quality area, a Chrysler manufacturing veteran named George F. Butts was asked to take charge as vice-president. He has monitored quality ever since, free to devote entire staffs at Chrysler plants to this area and bypass superiors with reports on quality—or the lack of it—to the top executives themselves.

The Matthias consultancy helped Iacocca by pinpointing another production whiz whose career had led to the vice-presidency for engines and castings, a Berlin native named Stephen Sharf. A tough-minded Jewish "Prussian," Sharf had been dead-ended by management, which had failed to reward his manufacturing expertise. Sharf was to rise to executive vice-president of Chrysler and emerge as one of only three old guard vice-presidents to stay on the new Iacocca team, the others being Butts and Glenn E. White, head of personnel and organization.

Iacocca faced more pressing problems than rebuilding Chrysler's organization the week he began work on Massachusetts Avenue, however. The 1979-model launch had started in the pits, and new cars and trucks were piling up again—built helter-skelter without regard for dealer orders. What would the new chief do to untangle this pattern—a replay of the nefarious "sales bank"? Iacocca flatly opposed this modus operandi, realizing that Chrysler's return to profitability hinged on erasure of the "sales bank" and its month-end distress sales to dealers once and for all. The veteran communicator typically took his case right to the Chrysler dealers, telling them that it would be their fault if the "sales bank" continued and the company went down the drain as a result.

First, the dealers would have to pitch in and help clean out the prodigious inventory clogging Chrysler's pipelines over the winter of 1978–79. Dealers could not take what they wanted "and to hell with the rest," he told Chrysler's "only customers." More of the same, and Chrysler was doomed, he implied.

Eventually, with Gar Laux inducted to oversee the overhaul, Chrysler dealers and sales personnel changed their ways to the Ford and GM style. "As a result," Iacocca said, "we no longer operate in a daily panic." Or on a rollercoaster, up one quarter and down the next.

Iacocca had completed Phase One. He had brought in Bergmoser, Laux, and Matthias. But he still was faced with the existing organization and the challenge of finding new blood to replace or supersede the carryover "losers."

Phase Two was at hand.

11

QUALITY—

OR ELSE

LESS THAN SIX MONTHS BEFORE HE LEFT FORD, Iacocca had unconsciously set the stage for Phase Two of his management build-up at Chrysler a year later. He had ordered up a ranked list of top Ford financial talent from J. Edward Lundy, Ford's powerful executive vice-president for finance.

Constant review of up-and-coming staff personnel was a trademark of Iacocca's management style. He compared his approach to that of a baseball manager, always evaluating reports of his farm-system managers, seeking hot players who might be overlooked and so neglected that they left for other teams.

At Ford, Iacocca had monitored the careers of

perhaps three hundred junior and senior executives. William Clay Ford, Henry's younger brother and company vice-chairman, gave Iacocca permission to take these confidential black books with him when he set sail for other shores in the fall of 1978, perhaps never dreaming that he would use these lists to staff Chrysler in the not-too-distant future. The journals included Lundy's gradings of junior finance executives, one of the most highly rated of whom was Gerald Greenwald, then forty-three and head of Ford of Venezuela.

Iacocca was drawn to Greenwald, who ambitiously had urged Lundy and his other seniors to let him try an operations post and branch out from finance. He was a Princeton economics graduate as well, making him a fellow alumnus of Iacocca's. And it didn't hurt that Greenwald was handsome and polished, characteristics that the rough-hewn Iacocca secretly admired.

On the other hand, several old Ford hands regarded Venezuela and assignments like it as dead-enders. The fact that Greenwald was Jewish could have been a handicap to Greenwald's advancement at Ford as well, since the company had never named a Jewish vice-president. Iacocca couldn't have cared less, having already singled out Steve Sharf at Chrysler for advancement in manufacturing out of a determination to pick the best and the brightest for the Chrysler team whatever their race or religion.

The Venezuela operation, which involved a manufacturing plant, had been run by Greenwald since 1976. He had increased profits there tenfold on a sales increase of nearly 300 percent, boosting Ford's vehicle market share from 28 to 37 percent—the highest of any Ford subsidiary. Clearly he was a man to bag, and Iacocca wasted no time in calling Caracas after determining that Greenwald combined operational know-how with financial expertise. He did not want a "bean counter," however worthy, if he lacked schooling in marketing and manufacturing.

Greenwald was reluctant to leave Ford, and it took the relentless Iacocca four months to sign him on as Chrysler's new comptroller. There were meetings in Miami and Las Vegas, with Greenwald insisting that he should have an operations assignment and Iacocca stressing the need to straighten out Chrysler's blurry financial picture first.

Finally, Iacocca, who has an amazing ability to get whom he wants, won Greenwald's assent. No less than Henry Ford II, William Clay Ford, and Philip Caldwell tried to talk Greenwald out of his defection, perhaps inwardly fearing it could open the conduits to the Iacocca-run operation across town. Greenwald told Henry Ford II that he was eager to take part in a corporate revival move, not unlike the one directed by Henry himself in the 1940s. Greenwald also said that he could not refuse an instant senior-management position that probably was years away at Ford. The Greenwald bolt from Ford, which did indeed touch off a one-way flow to Chrysler from Dearborn, was assured when Greenwald failed to get a counteroffer of a major position in overseas or finance.

There was something else compelling about going to work for Iacocca, even though Chrysler was such a zoo that one could well have asked, "Who needs it?" It wasn't money, because Chrysler's financial future was far from assured and the thorny issue of federal loan guarantees had not surfaced as yet. It wasn't power, because well-fixed retirees like Bergmoser, Laux, and Matthias all had reached the heights at Ford in their day, while Greenwald was comfortably fixed as the boss of Ford in Venezuela and could look forward to promotions to key posts in Ford's international staff.

In Greenwald's wake came a steady stream of experienced hands from, primarily, Ford and Volkswagen of America. It has been often said that without Iacocca, Chrysler might have submerged into chapter eleven or seven bankruptcy. But Iacocca readily realized that he could never save the waterlogged Chrysler with the crew that was already on board. It was incumbent on him to back up Greenwald and the already-seated Sperlich with a new crew up and down the line.

Like explorers setting out from comfortable villas and incomes in Spain and Italy with Christopher Columbus, they fell in behind Captain Iacocca.

Greenwald helped corral a Ford finance-staff associate, Robert S. (Steve) Miller, whose task became
to place the federally guaranteed loans with four
hundred wary banks. Gar Laux brought in two sharp
Ford sales executives, Jerry Pyle and Jack Givens.
A VW of America vice-president, Richard E. Dauch,
who had shepherded the Rabbit into assembly,
moved over into Chrysler manufacturing with a fist-
ful of young manufacturing managers. Bergmoser,
the purchasing veteran, recruited Ford's David Platt.
Public relations, a pet Iacocca function, was divided
between Baron K. Bates, a twenty-year VW of America publicist who had previously worked for Chrysler, and James. L. Tolley, vice-president of public
relations at American Motors who had also been a
GM public relations executive.

"They did it for the thrill and for Lee Iacocca,"
an observer has said. Possibly the order should be
reversed, because it was a fired-up Iacocca,
unleashed at last, who promised them the thrill in
whatever form—big money, big power, greater self-
esteem. They had nowhere to go but up—like
Chrysler stock, like Chrysler itself, even like a Ford
president rising from a nine-count knockdown.
Maybe, too, they were young enough to figure they
could land on their feet if Chrysler's cancer turned
out to be terminal.

By the first quarter of 1979, Iacocca and Bergmoser concluded that whatever could go wrong with
Chrysler's management structure had gone wrong.

Iacocca compared the situation to his parents' native Italy until 1860—a collection of small states balking at a single authority. He moaned, "Everybody has his own little empire—twenty little companies and no one to pull them together."

Centralized direction had had to be imposed throughout Ford, Iacocca recalled, reflecting a common industry malady. Chrysler's semiautonomous product engineering group, for example, had refused to cooperate with manufacturing—and vice versa. The resulting dispute more often than not involved the chairman or president of the corporation, a pattern from the K. T. Keller days and absolutely anathema to Iacocca.

Bergmoser, after reviewing the purchasing staff over the winter of 1979, gave Iacocca a diagnosis of Chrysler's illness: underspecialization. Townsend had liked his executives to shift from finance to manufacturing to purchasing and back to finance— establishing an orchestra of violinists who could also play flutes and beat drums. The problem to Bergmoser, who had cultivated purchasing at Ford like a breeder of thoroughbred hounds, was that Chrysler was stuffed with generalists who were jacks-of-all-trades and masters of none.

Iacocca summed up the Chrylser plight this way: "You don't ask a brain surgeon to deliver a baby." He wanted to run a hospital, not a department store where you sold men's suits one day and furniture the next.

Bergmoser set about to implant at Chrysler the Ford system, wherein purchasing agents stayed in place for years and years, wherein "every finance staffer was not a graduate engineer and every finance guy was not asked to run a plant somewhere." He was appalled to find that Chrysler purchasing's top three staffers had a combined total of six years' experience in buying parts and components.

Ironically, Iacocca and Greenwald had themselves departed from the superspecialist track at Ford. Iacocca had been a graduate engineer when he came to Ford, only to be lodged in marketing by his mentor, Charlie Beacham. Greenwald got out of finance for an all-things operations assignment, which would give him a broad experience resume that would be of special attractiveness to headhunter Iacocca, as it turned out.

The Chrysler problem was compounded by the unique role enjoyed by engineering. No chairman since Walter Chrysler had emulated GM or Ford in blending engineering with the rest of the company's staffs or groups. Engineering started out on a pedestal and stayed above it all—oblivious to the designers or the quality-control problems faced by manufacturing, doing their own thing and letting the chips fall where they may. The advent of Iacocca dramatized the long-standing schism between engineering and the rest of the corporation, as one defect after another popped up on the full-size R-body cars upon which Chairman Riccardo and his executive vice-president for sales, R. K. Brown, had hung their hopes for a massive cash infusion in 1979. The cars leaked, rattled, and came off the assembly line with sloppy paint and trim fits. Chrysler warranty costs were up to 30 percent greater than those of GM or Ford.

Working with consultant Hans Matthias, an often-disputatious UAW, and under the gun of the fired-up Iacocca, Vice-President George Butts cracked the whip at the plant level as no one had ever done in the history of Chrysler. Discovery of defects led to creation of quality task forces whose members for the first time knew their jobs might be severed if permanent remedies were not found for leaks, rattles, stallouts, and whatever. Said Matthias, "We must get people off the idea of laying down their part of the job and walking away. We have to keep verifying it's right all the way through."

In short, no more passing the buck and "signing off." Quality-control supervisors, responsible for nothing else, would act as watchdogs continuously, with their jobs and prospective bonuses riding on how well they performed. "The customer doesn't give a damn *why* he has a problem," Matthias reminded Chrysler technicians, "just that he has it."

The turnaround in Chrysler started, and could have ended, without any improvement in product quality. Suppliers were wrung into the process, as was labor after a year-long struggle overseen by the feisty Iacocca, with the view toward bringing out the do-or-die K-body compact cars as trouble-free as possible.

The hands-on Iacocca was compelled to badger old-line Chrylser suppliers and unionists during the years when Chrysler was battling for federal loan guarantees and sparring with a crew of mutinous lenders. As the K-cars arrived at the end of 1980, Chrysler could claim that its warranty costs had fallen slightly below those of Ford and were nearly comparable to GM's.

The quality-control hammer wielded by Iacocca did not miss Chrysler's suppliers. Bergmoser, declaring that quality-control supervisors were a bargain when contrasted with the fallout of sloppy quality, restored to purchasing a quality control staff previously lopped off by Riccardo and Cafiero.

The transplantings and implantings of the Iacocca landscrapers were taking root and producing results. The time had come to assure that the first all-new products bearing the Iacocca signature—the Plymouth Reliant (aptly named?) and the Dodge Aries K-cars—came of fruition on time and in solid shape for the acid test of consumer acceptance. Otherwise, all the crash programs would have been in vain and Chrysler would be a dead duck.

12

OUT OF THE

FIRST TRENCH

ASKED THE SECRET OF SUCCESSFUL AUTO-motive managements, a senior General Motors executive replied back in 1960, "Control. Dealer control. Product control. Labor control."

The same answer was given shortly afterward in Wolfsburg, West Germany, home of Volkswagen-werk, whose rear-engine Beetle subcompact at the time was dominating world markets.

"Control," said the VW official. "Too much democracy, and products come out late and poorly built. There's no central authority for receivables and payables. Supplies rule the roost, instead of the other way around."

The helter-skelter way of operating at Chrysler had so stunned Iacocca, even though Sperlich had warned him what to expect, that he claims he genuinely felt misgivings about enticing so many securely positioned executives away from well-run companies like Ford and VW. Iacocca's plight overcame these reservations, however, determined as he was to give the Chrysler rescue effort an all-out try. The first mission of all conquestees was clearcut: To impose controls, to turn the jungle into a dairy farm.

Greenwald, the first AI ("After Iacocca") to fly Ford's coop, found at Chrysler to his dismay that central financing was all but nonexistent in the accounts payable area. The comptroller's staff had allowed twenty-five or more departments to handle their own bills, ruling out any single thermostat for calculating the company's total costs.

Not the least of these runaway costs was vehicle warranties, which wound up costing Chrysler up to $330 million a year. Ed Lundy's finance staff at Ford rode herd over such a potentially costly area as warranties, making sure that those in charge of approval of warranty claims from dealers and regional offices knew that they were under the factory's gun and couldn't wink at spurious claims.

Greenwald's effort to isolate warranty problems and pinpoint where the money was going to repair them met with a typical response at Chrysler. No one could tell Greenwald which ten warranty problems were costing the most, because a system to uncover these numbers simply did not exist. Sperlich had discovered this even before Iacocca found it out for himself. It was back to Business School Economics 101 for the free spirits in Chrysler finance, Greenwald thought.

Once having straightened the mess out in the comptroller's office and also having assured Sperlich's product development staff that new-model launches would henceforth be spared funding bottlenecks, Greenwald asked Iacocca to deliver on his promise of added duties. "Find yourself as good a comptroller as you are," Iacocca told Greenwald, "and you'll get other things to do."

Greenwald then, in the summer of 1979, prevailed on Steve Miller to leave as Ford of Venezuela finance director and enroll at Chrysler. The unflappable duo for Greenwald and Miller would keep all of Chrysler's banks on board during the loan bailout negotiations of 1980 and 1981 and, in Iacocca's words, "Chrysler could not have survived without them."

Untangling the mess in financial controls contributed to ending the inexcusable product-launch delays that had plagued Chrysler through the Riccardo and Cafiero years. Cafiero had been a notorious procrastinator on basic design decisions, partly because of his personality but also because there was no hesitation about overrunning budgets. The most flagrant example occurred just as Iacocca,

Bergmoser, Matthias, and company move in. The long-awaited full-size R-body cars were delayed a full four months because of Cafiero-dictated alterations, with dealer shipments failing to materialize until January in some cases—after an October preview!

Keeping to a budget and to a timetable are basic to the auto industry's annual parade of new models. "You can never make up for lost time," Bergmoser asserted. "Management discipline, or the lack of it, is all the difference in the world."

Yet strict control of schedules had been practiced at Chrysler in the 1950s and 1960s, an executive recalled, just as it had been at GM and Ford. "We had dates for everything—design of fenders or door trim or whatever, pilot production, preassembly." Adherence to schedules simply slipped from top priority to no priority in the waning years of the Townsend-Riccardo regimes, causing costly delays as the weak central finance staff itself became indifferent.

To admit, as an embittered John Riccardo did, that "we missed the launch" was no consolation to Iacocca and his product "Prussians" from Ford. That exercise in self-destruction could no more be repeated than the chaos in finances—or the habit of sliding over new-model delays and mistakes by shoving vehicle inventories down dealer throats out of sales banks. The cancer had metastasized through the entire system.

As Gar Laux surveyed the dealer network, he also uncovered erosion in central discipline. Dealers had been allowed to stay in business or to expand without regard for changing neighborhoods, because the factory's inept product launches required a maximum count of retail outlets to siphon off the constant sales bank crises. Chrysler's 4800 dealers were able to average only about three hundred new-car sales a year on a company share of 10 percent of the total market, compared with five hundred a year at Ford and six hundred at GM. The profits of the Chrysler dealers were hurt by the excessive intramural competition in metropolitan markets, as Laux learned, as well as by the nearly two hundred factory-owned stores carried over from Townsend's regime, which operated as volume pumpers in direct competition with the privately owned dealers. A company-owned dealership, Laux told Iacocca, "is just about as unfair a form of competition as I know—and simply unloads cars without generating profits for the stores or the factory." By the end of 1980, with Iacocca's blessing, Laux's sales staff had sold to private owners or folded all but thirty-five company stores, and there are only a handful left today.

Discipline, lacking in finance and product development, was also lacking in sales administration, Laux discovered. A central staff over the sales department more or less existed, but it usually left regions or districts without regular instructions and almost totally ignorant of what other areas were doing or not doing. The breakdown in communications in part resulted from the fact that Chrysler relied for the bulk of its sales volume on about 2000 of its 4800 dealers, through whom flowed more than four of every five sales. (Six hundred dealers did half the business, far more than the ratios at GM or Ford.) The volume dealers called the shots—a messy kettle of fish for the Ford-trained Laux staffers who had learned to appreciate the role of smaller-volume dealers in outlying towns in maintaining Ford's reputation and public awareness.

As with other Chrysler departments, the marketing staff got and spent its money without a comptroller on hand to keep tabs on excesses or past experiences. Greenwald, discovering in mid-1979 that exchanges between the finance staff and all operating staffs were few and far between, pinpointed the root cause as the lack of highly motivated auditors or accountants in Chrysler finance. Laux said the gap between finance and marketing stemmed from the common malady in the Chrysler modus operandi: "No discipline."

Why would Chrysler's "bean counters" have been so remiss? One explanation given Greenwald and Iacocca was that ex-accountants Townsend and Riccardo understood the intricacies of budgets so well that they didn't need back-up financial analysis. Iacocca, with Greenwald concurring, decided early on to institute the stringent GM and Ford money monitoring techniques at Chrysler with minimal delay. The scattershot system had to end, if for no other reason (and there were plenty of others) than to satisfy federal loan guarantee administrators and their congressional overseers if and when Chrysler sought bailout funds from a skeptical Washington.

In order to remold the Chrysler finance staff, Greenwald was compelled to do battle against the toughest of all handicaps when major organizational surgery is diagnosed—a shortage of funds. Close to 8500 "deadwood" white-collar employees had been sacked or early-retired in the first half of 1979, leaving the financial staff as lean as most others, just as the new comptroller set about to reassign the survivors to operating departments.

But Greenwald proved equal to the task, and the result was what Iacocca set about to instill throughout Chrysler management. He wanted to remake each aspect of Chrysler into a self-perpetuating entity of its own, graded against comparable departments at other automakers, with independent budgets, profits, and losses. It was the kind of accountability familiar to even nonincome-producing GM and Ford activities like styling and public relations. At Chrysler, it was the dark side of the moon.

"Unless you know the costs," said Iacocca, "you'll be noncompetitive against not only GM and Ford but the importers and on parts, the aftermarket guys.

You've also got to know investments and you've got to know accounted profit."

Iacocca's cost probers uncovered inefficiency after inefficiency, however, the legacy of a prolonged period of neglect. There were up to 110 separate driveshaft combinations on trucks, literally thousands of paint combinations, duplications on replacement parts— all tremendously cost-consuming. "Productivity," Iacocca stressed, "gets shot to hell on complexity or short runs. You make money not with a potful of options and parts, but with long runs and spin-offs of existing models and platforms."

Iacocca spoke with the benefit of much experience on this score. The 1964 Ford Mustang really was an offshoot, with fancier exterior styling, of the "plain jane" 1960 Ford Falcon subcompact. It used the same four-cylinder engine and transmission— and made Ford millions of dollars. Iacocca's expertise in adapting and converting was implemented to the nth degree at Chrysler, when the K-body compacts provided the platform for the subsequent "stretched" sedans, sports coupes, and even minivans—all carrying the same 2.2-liter four-cylinder engine and front-drive transmission!

While Sperlich's technicians toiled night and day under Iacocca's scrutiny to give birth to the best Plymouth Reliant K and Dodge Aries K possible in the fall of 1980, the chairman-to-be kept at his overall mission of trying to retrench and rebuild the company. The Shah of Iran's flight in January 1979 had revived the energy supply fears of 1974–75, slashing big-car sales but giving a boost to Chrylser's smaller Colts, Omnis, and Horizons—and providing a timely preface to the four-cylinder K-cars if only Chrysler could hang on that long.

With the beginning of the Iranian oil cutoff and the uncertainties it begat on the world auto situation, Iacocca found it more difficult than he expected to lure additional key staffers away from Ford. He did recruit Lincoln and VW assembly plant managers, but the big surprise conquest was not another Greenwald or Sperlich but, as of March 1, 1979, one of Ford's major advertising agencies—New York-based Kenyon & Eckhardt, which would displace longtime Chrysler agencies Young & Rubicam and Batten Barton Durstine & Osborne. K & E would take over all $120 million worth of Chrysler's car, truck, and corporate advertising.

K & E had been associated with Ford since 1945 and its defection to the Iacocca fold, engineered by the Chrysler president's long personal relationship with K & E executives John Morrissey and Arthur Kelmenson, came as a shock to Ford. It was K & E whose "Sign of the Cat" pitch for the Mercury car consistently won consumer recognition awards over *all* other makes. The "Ford Has a Better Idea" line came from the K & E creative department. "I feel," chortled the baseball-loving Iacocca, "like I just bought the New York Yankees."

In guaranteeing his new agency $120 million in

annual billings, Iacocca also effectively cut the total Chrysler ad layout from $150 million. And for the first time he lumped Dodge and Chrysler-Plymouth together under one ad umbrella and switched signals on Laux, who believed that Dodge and Chrysler-Plymouth should be divorced in every area of marketing, like Chevrolet and Pontiac or Ford and Lincoln-Mercury.

Crisis followed crisis in 1979, testing Iacocca like an inner-city emergency-room surgeon working seven days a week. The Iranian revolution led to a prodigious pileup of full-size and mid-size Chrysler cars by late March, inducing R. K. Brown, as executive vice-president for sales, to resort to an old Chrysler ploy of hustling the stock through boiler-room phone calls by factory staffers in the last ten-day period of March. Dealers knew what was coming and ordered the distress merchandise at cut-rate prices like there was no tomorrow. Fully 66,423 vehicles were sold by Chrysler March 21–31, 1979, more than doubling the normal ten-day volume and still an all-time company record.

"It was the biggest shock of my life," Iacocca said of the month-end sales explosion. "I almost threw the towel in early." It was too late for surrender, though, and he knew it, realizing inwardly that the coup in landing the prestigious Kenyon & Eckhardt ad agency had dramatically helped change the despondent mood among Chrysler dealers to the buoyancy reflected in those record sales.

Indeed, the transfusion of Chrysler was progressing at a faster clip than even Iacocca had forecast. The all-new crew was taking shape as the 1980 models approached and with them the end of the benighted 1970s decade for the number-three automaker, which some analysts had switched from the Big Three to the Little Three.

Still to be overcome by Iacocca was the horrendous money crunch and the grave doubts as to Chrysler's survivability even if everything suddenly were to come Chrysler's way. Iacocca was out of the first trench, but no man's land still lay before him.

13

IACOCCA BITES
THE BULLET

WHEN PRESIDENT JIMMY CARTER SIGNED the Chrysler Corporation Loan Guarantee Act of 1979 on January 7, 1980, Chrysler Chairman Lee Iacocca had won a turning-point battle in the fight to save the company. It had been a year like no other experienced by a chief executive of a major corporation, testing Iacocca constantly like a Marine commander leading his forces through a course of endless obstacles, anyone of which could have repelled the assault.

Yet the attainment of the bailout guarantee package from the federal government in actuality guaranteed Chrysler nothing by itself. A formidable array of conditions and concessions faced Chrysler before Iacocca could see his way clear and breathe easy about the future of the corporation. It had taken him a solid year to nail down the Normandy beachhead. It would require three more years to restore Chrysler to full strength.

As President Iacocca sought to bring order out of chaos in Chrysler's operational structure in early 1979, Chairman Riccardo reported a first-quarter loss of $53.8 million and warned that losses would escalate so steeply by the end of the year that a massive bailout would be mandatory to prevent the company from formally going bankrupt.

News that Chrysler was in extremis sent shock waves throughout the four hundred banks to which the company owed money, particularly the smaller banks. There were, in addition, outstanding loans of $251 million to Prudential Insurance Co., $70 million to Aetna Life, and $50 million in notes to Blue Cross/Blue Shield. The small banks, to which Chrysler owed about $70 million, feared that they would be the last to be repaid in any bailout package or eventual bankruptcy. Many of these smaller banks demanded immediate payment of their loans— meeting a flat Chrysler turndown.

Chrysler's deepening financial crisis, which complicated Iacocca's efforts to revamp the organization with new outside talent, was played out against the backdrop of a national gasoline shortage. The situation was aggravated by federal standards requiring cars to use lead-free gasoline while at the same time improving their mileage-per-gallon capability.

President Carter, with gasoline prices soaring, called on April 1, 1979, for a windfall profits tax on oil producers and decontrol of oil prices over a period of years. Gasoline lines—for the second time in five years—flared up in California. The nation was preoccupied again with a situation over which it had no control, but one that held the threat of changing life-styles dramatically.

How could the financially strapped Chrysler, whose cars had plunged so abysmally in quality reputation, hope to win support for an unprecedented federal loan guarantee package? Absent Iacocca, Chrysler would have been allowed to go the chapter eleven bankruptcy route in that hectic 1979–80 period—a course that would have nailed the coffin airtight, as Iacocca said later, because sales would have dried up and dealers would have deserted to rival makes.

One of Chrysler's mainstays in auto sales recessions had been its Dodge truck business. Proliferation of vans and utility vehicles in the mid-1970s, spurred by the boom in recreational traveling and camping, was a significant plus for Chrysler, the principal supplier of engines and powertrains to such van giants as Winnebago. Collapse of big-van sales in the spring of 1979, a victim of the gasoline shortfall, materially deepened Chrysler's profits and sales slump. Sales of economical diesel-engine cars and trucks rallied, with GM benefiting as a builder of V-8 diesel-engine cars, but Chrysler's cash crunch had forced it to steer clear of a diesel program in what Iacocca described as a typical example of "penny-wise, pound-foolish" product planning.

With confidence—at least outwardly—that Chrysler would survive the impending financial disaster, Iacocca ordered Sperlich to accelerate development of the front-wheel-drive minivan, which would use the powertrain of the year-away K-body compact cars. Iacocca was not about to abort programs in the manner of previous chairmen when faced with sales downturns. The minivan had been Sperlich's "Holy Grail" product even back in his Ford days, only to encounter vetoes because of fears it would cannibalize from the larger one-ton vans. The Chrysler minivan finally appeared in late 1983 and proved to be a big seller, as Iacocca and Sperlich had forecast when skeptical congressmen and lenders pondered the bailout package in late 1979.

The swing to small econocars in early 1979 did boost sales of Chrysler's Plymouth Horizon and Dodge Omni subcompacts, though profits on American-made cars in that segment have remained minuscule at best. The 1.7-liter four-cylinder engine powering the Omni and Horizon came from Volkswagen, whose domestic Rabbit used the same powerplant and was also a hot item at the time. VW refused to sell Iacocca more than the 300,000 engines promised in the 1979 model year, a constraint he determined would be lifted as soon as Chrysler could afford to do so. (Subsequently, Chrylser replaced the VW engine with its own 2.2-liter four-cylinder engine from 1981-model K-cars and a 1.6-liter four-cylinder from its French partner Peugeot. Living by the moods and necessities of outside suppliers is not one of Iacocca's favorite pastimes.)

The 1979 gasoline shortage came as a windfall for the small cars from Japan, raising their sales and U.S. market penetration to record levels and, in retrospect, establishing the Japanese presence as a dynamic, permanent force instead of a modest import factor. Shipments of Chrysler's own small-car imports, the Mitsubishi-built Colts, were limited by Mitsubishi after the Plymouth Horizon and Dodge Omni appeared and dealers tended to concentrate more on the domestic products.

It's hard to believe today, but Japanese cars were stacked up to a five-month supply at the Pacific Coast ports of entry on the day the Shah fled in January 1979. No one was paying premiums over suggested retail prices to obtain delivery of a Toyota Corolla or Honda Civic. And no one, least of all Iacocca, was screaming about trade imbalances with Japan or the artificial value of the yen against the dollar.

GM, always the omnipotent automaker that had kept Iacocca on his toes at Ford and Chrysler, also shouldered its way into the Chrysler opera during that eventful spring of 1979. Out fortuitously came economical X-car compacts from four of GM's five divisions "as if," Iacocca lamented, "God had touched them on the shoulder." The Chevrolet Citation, Pontiac Phoenix, Buick Skylark, and Oldsmobile Omega boasted a new 2.5-liter four-cylinder engine and that new powertrain rage—front-wheel drive. The GM quartet added to Chevrolet's traditional small-car clout the stature of Buick, Oldsmobile, and Pontiac dealers with their own X-car versions.

Chrysler's front-wheel-drive compacts were more than a year away, and Ford's were further than that. GM had the front-wheel-drive four-cylinder "family car" market to itself, except for the surging Japanese. Chrysler found itself with shrinking working capital as sales and profits deteriorated in the second quarter of 1979, increasing the inventory of unsold vehicles to a bloated count of nearly 50,000 and threatening to reignite the sales bank–type clearance that had been successful as recently as the end of March.

Iacocca, backed by Gar Laux, decided once and for all to end that type of operation. Dealers were offered wholesale incentives and production was slashed, but whether they liked it or not, and most dealers had lived no other way, the cycles of waiting for dumping bees by the factory every three or four months were to be ended. Chrysler dealers reluctantly changed their ways because Iacocca knew the factory had the ultimate "hammer" as the franchiser, and he was not averse to seeing the company lose several hundred "spoiled" franchisees to reduce an excessive number of retail outlets.

A countermeasure against GM's X-cars and the onrushing Japanese was the revival by Iacocca of the five-year 50,000-mile engine and transmission warranty—still a Chrysler across-the-product-line exclusive feature. But Iacocca was forced to inflict more drastic retrenchment measures on the Chrysler corpus, while Riccardo begged for banker indulgences.

At the outset of a pruning exercise that he as an outsider could perform without sentimental attachments, Iacocca ordered the closing of the Dodge main plant in Hamtramck by June 1980. Dodge Main had served as the production heart of Chrysler, employing in its heyday as many as 33,000 workers. The "Dotch," as its Polish-born workers called it, was to Chrysler as Rouge was to Ford or Flint Buick to GM. Iacocca knew, however, that the multistoried Dodge Main, where the low-quality rear-drive Dodge Aspen and Plymouth Volare compacts were being assembled, was too expensive to consider modernizing. It had to go, and he had to unload it.

By September 18, 1979, when the haggard Riccardo resigned and Iacocca became chairman and chief executive officer, the cost-reduction program had reached about $350 million in less than a year's time. Unlike the comparable economy drives of

Iacocca's predecessors, nothing was extracted from the future-products program, and Sperlich was given carte blanche to hire whomever he needed or to spend whatever he required to develop the products for Chrylser's resurgence. Iacocca boosted the monthly new-product budget from $100 million to $160 million. What good would it do to receive renewed loans from lenders and even a federal bailout law, he argued, if products were being upstaged by the competition?

This was the hallmark of Iacocca at the helm: beg, borrow, and steal for product out of the other branches on the tree. Tooling for the 1981-model K-cars had to be ordered in the summer and fall of 1979, and it was agreed to automate the aged Chrysler Jefferson Avenue plant on Detroit's lower east side at a prodigious cost for the K-body Plymouth Reliant and Dodge Aries.

Meanwhile, Sperlich's product men were touching up as much as they could the downsized Chrysler Cordoba and Dodge Miranda intermediate cars due in the fall of 1979—they would be the first of the "Iacocca Regime." In no way could they appear with the catastrophic results of the full-size R-body cars a year earlier.

Behind the scenes, the pot was cooking for private rescue attempts at Chrysler. No chief officer at a major corporation as financially squeezed as Chrysler was could realistically shrug off private-sector proposals for mergers or restructurings, simply because a federal bailout was in the realm of "mission impossible" and business was going from bad to worse to near-fatal.

A seriously proposed merger with Volkswagen was discussed in 1979 for many hours and at many different locales. VW walked away eventually, although Iacocca had been a strong advocate of the tieup, ostensibly because the West German automaker shrank from Chrysler's financial plight, but partly because of fear that Iacocca would be too strong-minded a leader to bend to the will of the barons in VW headquarters at Wolfsburg.

A private bailout plan, conceived by New York investment banker Felix Rohatyn, was summarily rejected by Riccardo and the Chrysler board. Rohatyn, who had helped stitch together Renault's 46.1 percent investment in American Motors and who serves on AMC's board, angered both Riccardo and Iacocca by insisting as part of the Chrysler reorganization and refinancing that he become chairman of the Chrysler finance committee and possibly chairman down the road. Ironically, the Rohatyn plan was quite similar to the one set up in 1980 after passage of the federal loan guarantee act.

Late in June 1979, *Automotive News*, the same automotive trade paper that had broken the story of Henry Ford II's sacking of Iacocca a year earlier, ran another front-page scoop: VW was to propose a takeover of Chrysler for $15 a share, below Chrysler's book value of $40 a share. Treasury Secretary

Michael Blumenthal, meeting Riccardo the day after the story broke, urged him to accept the reported "offer." But the "offer," if there ever was one, had been withdrawn. VW executives have refused to confirm the story.

Chrysler's second-quarter loss in 1979 reached $207 million and, far from depleting the stockpile of unsold cars, Iacocca's abolition of the sales bank had mushroomed the albatross inventory as of June 30 to a whopping 75,000 vehicles.

It was do-or-die, the free-enterprise predilections of the pillars of American government, industry, and labor be damned. Chrysler, driven by one of the most flamboyantly aggressive executives in American industry, would go after the last thing such a freewheeler ever would want or need—help from Washington.

14

THE "LEADER"

GETS A BAILOUT

BAILOUT—OR BANKRUPTCY. THOSE WERE the choices facing the fifty-five-year-old Chrysler Corporation and its new fifty-five-year-old chairman, Lee Iacocca, in the fall of 1979. Never in American history had the federal government been asked to rescue a consumer-product manufacturer of such size, or of any size for that matter.

It was a "precedent" all right, to use a much-overworked word, running smack against the grain of the American free-enterprise system. There had been bailouts for Penn Central and Lockheed, but this one was different. This one bordered on state socialism. It was opposed by liberals like Ralph Nader and Senator Gary Hart, as well as by conservatives like GM Chairman Thomas A. Murphy, who declared that "there should never be a guarantee that anyone is insulated from competition," and "there's never been a business that was viable that lacked financing."

Given the opposition, ranging from the predictably hostile *Wall Street Journal* to the usually sympathetic *New York Times* and *Washington Post*, one can only marvel at how Iacocca orchestrated the federal bailout victory. Riccardo stepped down from the Chrysler helm to clear the way for the make-or-break drive on the federal establishment (or, failing that, for a chapter eleven bankruptcy petition that would be Iacocca's to file.) It was not a struggle for which even the normally aggressive Iacocca had been schooled, but who had been trained ever before for such an assault?

Business school professors, like Harvard's respected Abraham Zaleznik, regard Iacocca and executives like him as "leaders" rather than "managers." The "leaders" of the Iacocca ilk provoke drama and change by their very natures, often unpredictably. They do not shrink from seizing the moment for course reversals. To Dr. Zaleznik, the Iacoccas of the business world "are often obsessed by their ideas, which appear visionary and consequently excite, stimulate and drive other people to work hard and create reality out of fantasy."

By contrast, the Zaleznik theory categorizes cor-

porate managers as believers in "process" and in the
organization. GM's modern-day founder and revered
former chairman, Alfred P. Sloan, Jr., epitomizes the
manager type, according to Zaleznikists, who would
add Tom Murphy but raise a doubt or two about the
present chairman, Roger B. Smith, a groundbreaker
for GM who has demonstrated a knack for turning
dreams of outside acquisition and expansion into
reality.

Could a "manager" named Lynn Townsend or
Philip Caldwell have brought off a bailout á la
Chrysler? Or did it require the charisma engendered by the leadership of Iacocca, who could mus-
ter labor and political allies to march in lockstep
with his vision of a "new" and resurgent Chrysler?

The vast majority of successful big-business top
executives dispute the contention that no happy
medium exists between a "leader" and a "manager."
They argue that a chairman can manage and motivate at the same time, either by personality impact
or by finding a stimulator as needed in the organization.

But according to University of Southern California Professor Warren Bennis, you're either an Iacocca
type or you aren't, and role-switchers are few and
far between. The reason lies in the deep-seated class
division between corporate and entrepreneurial eth-
ics, he explains, and in the difficulty of ruling an
industrial corporate roost like a free spirit running
a movie studio.

What Iacocca had to instill in the government and public as Chrysler pursued its bailout package was a "vision" transcending the simple issue of keeping alive a failing company whose management had been inept. To be sure, thousands of jobs and dealerships would be lost with a Chrysler collapse, but many of the displaced would go elsewhere, and "that's the system, isn't it?"

As *The New York Times* editorialized, "Bailing out failing companies is a route the British have pursued with disastrous results. It is not a path the United States needs to follow." *The Washington Post* asserted that foreign cars "offer a stronger guarantee of future competition than a weak domestic company propped up by public subsidies." This was heavy stuff from two progressive "bibles," reflecting the obstacle course faced by a dreamer even of Iacocca's impressive stature.

Iacocca may strike business school professors as a consummate "leader" with a crusader's zeal to reach the Promised Land. But he is nothing if not a pragmatist when it comes to assembling the right people for the immediate operation at hand. It's a two-way street, this business of conducting or administering, and musicians who'll play their hearts out for a conductor like Toscanini will coast along playing the same symphony for a lesser light.

To get federal help, Iacocca was required to present Congress with a cast of principals inspired by his baton. There was no time to waste, moreover, because Chrysler was running out of cash to pay its bills and that guillotine—chapter eleven—had to be avoided at all costs.

At first, Chrysler was shot down on two prebailout proposals, one for exemption from government auto emissions deadlines, the other for a special tax credit. A key figure in warning Chrysler Chairman Riccardo away from either avenue was UAW President Fraser, who sensed that neither idea would fly in Washington and—showing marketing astuteness that attracted him to Iacocca as a potential Chrysler director—who told Riccardo that neither would do much to buoy the company's lagging vehicle sales.

The meetings between Riccardo and Fraser, held before Iacocca assumed the chairmanship in September 1979, did have several positive vibes for Chrysler later. Fraser, politically the most astute president in UAW history, was brought into the management process and thus made a key figure in the lobbying ahead for the loan guarantee bill. An immediate side effect was the UAW decision to formally drop Chrysler as a strike target for the 1979 contract negotiations, which wound up with GM and Ford tightening Chrysler's financial squeeze by agreeing to the costliest wage and fringe-benefit settlements in automotive history.

The tax credit proposal did not die a-borning, actually. Several prominent congressional and administration officials endorsed it in the summer of 1979, not least of whom were Treasury Secretary Blumenthal, a former chairman of the major automotive supplier Bendix, and the powerful chairman of the Senate Finance Committee, Senator Russell E. Long, Louisiana Democrat.

Political winds and crosswinds, like acts of God and falls of Iranian Shahs, upended the tax credit ploy. President Carter fired Blumenthal on July 19, 1979, piqued at the disagreements between the Cabinet officer and Carter's White House advisers. Blumenthal's successor, former Federal Reserve Board Chairman G. William Miller, flatly rejected the tax credit idea at his swearing-in press conference.

Fortunately for Chrysler, Miller did favor the loan guarantee concept, though not above $750 million. A crusty former chairman of Textron, Miller had taken a dislike to Riccardo, whom he thought second-rate, and as FRB chief had bluntly told Riccardo to reorganize Chrysler under chapter eleven of the bankruptcy code if the lenders finally closed the loan window.

In switching the survival remedy from tax credits to loan guarantees, however, Miller threw Chrysler from friends to foes in Congress. Senator Long could expedite tax relief, which had been approved for American Motors in 1968, but the chairmen of the committees through which a loan guarantee bill would have to be steered were "antis" all the way: Senator William Proxmire, Wisconsin Democrat, and

Representative Henry Reuss, also a Wisconsin Democrat.

Furthermore, Chrysler's already-precarious cash position, which had forced August pay cuts of 2 percent to 5 percent for about 1700 salaried workers, would be hard pressed to absorb interest rates on new loans at prevailing percentages of nearly 11 percent.

Nor were loan guarantees Iacocca's number-one choice, although with typical enthusiasm he set about masterminding the drive to win congressional approval and put his magnetic personality solidly behind the effort. Wendell (Lars) Larsen, Chrysler's public relations vice-president then and a Riccardo intimate, had taken charge of the federal rescue project and was kept in place after Iacocca rose to the Chrysler chairmanship. Iacocca's formal presence as chairman, Larsen has said, assured passage of the controversial guarantee bill. It was a triumph of "leadership" over "management."

The first concrete test of Iacocca's chairmanship came with UAW negotiations in September and October 1979. The administration in Washington had backed loan guarantees for Chrylser, but enabling legislation was put on hold until Chrysler and the UAW could resolve the problem of the new GM-Ford contracts. Iacocca wanted substantial concessions from the union, representing a departure from the usually solid front between the Big Three automakers and the UAW. Fraser was sympathetic, but selling the workers on taking less than their brethren at GM and Ford would prove tough.

Once again, the "strong leader" mystique prevailed over entrenched principles. The Chrysler workers swallowed some $203 million in concessions, plus a $100 million deferred payment to the pension fund. In exchange, Iacocca would nominate Fraser to the Chrysler board in the spring of 1980.

The liaison between automotive management and labor gave the administration, worried about Carter's 1980 reelection chances, a green light to drive all-out on the Chrysler expressway. Vice-President Mondale and a young Michigan member of the House Banking Committee, Representative James Blanchard (now governor of Michigan), took key roles. Treasury Secretary Miller was reluctant at first, sending Chrysler officers and directors back several times to scale back its loan guarantee ceiling and increase its lost retrenchment commitment.

Finally, after Chrysler brought members of Congress and administration leaders a detailed prospectus showing photos of all future products with profit margins and management salaries spelled out in detail, President Carter announced the good news: The administration would seek passage of a Chrysler-only loan guarantee bill providing for a $1.5 billion ceiling—twice what Treasury Secretary Miller had endorsed.

Miller did an about-face, reportedly after a secret

meeting with Iacocca, who warned him direly what a bankruptcy would mean to federally funded welfare payments, federal and state taxes, and—on the bottom line—to Carter's reelection chances. Chrysler estimated that the cost of added welfare payments in the collapse of Chrysler (since few believed Chrysler could emerge from protracted bankruptcy litigation) could reach $1.5 billion alone, compounded by an annual tax loss of up to $500 million. Out of work would be more than 110,000 hourly Chrysler workers and out of business would be 19,000 suppliers and 4000 Chrysler dealers, together with their employees!

Bankruptcy would redound on an already-savaged Carter, who was facing a renomination threat from Senator Edward M. Kennedy and thereafter the likelihood of a rough race against the Republicans' Ronald Reagan. Miller then used the "pain and suffering" argument in his statement of support for loan guarantees, one that had not entered his reactions to the proposal before.

With politics rearing its head and the Christmas recess approaching, followed by the quadrennial Presidential primaries, there was no time to waste in pushing loan guarantees through Congress. Iacocca, aided by Fraser and Detroit Mayor Coleman Young, accelerated their lobbying efforts as soon as bills were introduced in the House and Senate. The bills called on Chrysler to raise another $1.5 billion from suppliers, lenders, dealers, employees, and state and local governments as a condition for "qualifying" for the $1.5 billion in federal loan guarantees—a seemingless prodigious task but one that Iacocca testified would not prove burdensome.

Even though several critics in Congress reacted negatively to what they called Iacocca's "hucksterism," the legislation moved relatively smoothly. Mayor Young had been one of the first black leaders to endorse Carter for the Presidency and—as they say—Carter "owed him one." Fraser's A-plus standing with rank-and-file workers sewed up many members of congress who otherwise might have balked at loan guarantees, since the Republicans already were beginning to make waves among the blue-collar voters disenchanted with Carter.

Finally, as Iacocca pointed out, Chrysler did have new leadership that needed the loan *guarantees* (*not* direct loans from the feds) to stand a chance of bouncing back to full health. Chrysler brought in delegations of dealers and suppliers to pressure their local Congressmen, though many philosophically bridled at federal bailouts. "Help us stay in business and give Iacocca a chance" was their message on Capitol Hill.

On the Tuesday before Christmas, the Chrysler loan guarantee bill passed the House by a vote of 271 to 136. The Senate, where Proxmire and a legion of antibailout Republicans held fast, insisting until the end on a three-year wage freeze stoutly opposed by Iacocca, and in the end settling for $462.5 million in union concessions instead, approved the measure by 53 to 44.

A relieved and recharged Iacocca called an unusual pre-Christmas Saturday press conference in the Chrysler headquarters building. He had charmed the reluctant dragon as no one before in American history. Success was far from assured, but the feds were committed.

"Let's go shopping," he said at the end of the conference. He already had the biggest gift of all.

15

WIELDING THE AXE—

TURNAROUND!

THE "NEW" CHRYSLER CORPORATION CAME into being the day President Carter signed the Chrysler Corporation Loan Guarantee Act into law on January 7, 1980. With the arrival of the decade of the 1980s came the unshackling of the Chrysler chairman, now financially free at last to show Henry Ford II and the world at large whether he could rebuild the all-but-lifeless auto giant.

For Iacocca, the litmus test of a lifetime was poised to begin. True, he would be "reporting to" a Loan Guarantee Board composed of three top-level U.S. government officials—the secretary of the treasury, the chairman of the Federal Reserve Board, and the comptroller of the currency—but now Chrysler was his to make or break. The feds could guarantee up to $1.5 billion in loans, but they couldn't induce dealers or consumers to buy whatever vehicles the Iacocca team saw fit to hurl into the tough American market.

There remained several roadblocks under the law for Chrysler to surmount before the federal loan guarantees could be formalized. The way Iacocca and his senior financial staffers, Gerry Greenwald and Steve Miller, cleared these obstacles in the early months of 1980 demonstrated clearly that the new Chrysler Corporation had been molded for success and not wheelspinning or failure.

Here was the list of financial "musts" facing Chrysler:

1. Existing U.S. lenders were obliged to extend $400 million in new credit and $100 million in concessions on existing loans.
2. Foreign lenders were asked to extend an added $150 million in credit.
3. Chrysler would raise $300 million through the sale of additional assets.
4. Suppliers were to furnish at least $180 million, of which $100 million would emanate from stock purchases in Chrysler.
5. State and local governments where Chrysler had manufacturing operations were required to advance at least $250 million in funds.

6. New stock worth $50 million would be sold to the public.
7. Concessions of $462.2 million would be asked of Chrysler union employees and $125 million from salaried employees.

It was quite an obstacle course, but a determined Iacocca and Greenwald tackled the problems in a methodical fashion. Twenty-two "work teams" were quickly created to deal with the specific target areas: local governments, suppliers, investment firms, the UAW, the banks, and so forth. Reports were presented every Friday in what often led to marathon sessions running into Saturday morning, when attack points were delineated for the following week.

Strangely, the banks turned out to be the toughest nuts to crack, and the UAW and key state governments the easiest. By the end of January, Fraser's UAW had wangled rank-and-file approval of the necessary concessions, barely months after winning ratification of the first concessionary package.

Suppliers followed suit with their own price rollbacks and Chrysler stock purchases, no surprise because a failure on the part of the assembler would doom many of them, too. Several states held out longer than expected, mostly on philosophical grounds, but essentially states and cities where Chrysler plants were situated had little choice politically but to help the troubled employer.

The banks were another story. It took Chrysler

longer to obtain $1.5 billion in loan guarantees from its 442 bank lenders than to push the loan guarantee bill through Congress. Chrysler needed the impossible, furthermore: the unanimous approval of all its bank lenders. Greenwald called the unanimity sine qua non "preposterous," and indeed 100 percent acceptance from a group of suspicious and obdurate bankers might never have fabricated had it not been for the pressure applied by Iacocca himself.

For a company that had always wooed banks and that at one time counted as many as twelve of its twenty-three directors on boards of big banks or financial institutions, the reluctance of several of its lenders to advance more money—despite federal guarantees—came as a bitter pill. The opposition bloc was centered on smaller banks, some in Chrysler plant cities like St. Louis, which raised questions as to how their additional loans to Chrysler would be "guaranteed" and added to Greenwald's concern over the company's immediate cash-flow status, which was wrenchingly bleak.

In fact, unless Chrysler could implement the Loan Guarantee Act by April 1, 1980, the bankers were warned at first by Greenwald and Miller that bankruptcy petitions were inevitable. At one point, the Chrysler finance chief stared at $800 million in upcoming bills with a cash-on-hand total of only $100 million. Delayed supplier payments and instant Band-Aid-type loans from the state of Michigan and the French partner Peugeot tided Chrysler over the first few of the threatened executions, but the small banks continued to procrastinate, forcing Chrysler to miss an April 1 deadline for availing itself of federal protection for new loans. More "instant fixes" were required as the deadline dragged on.

Iacocca orchestrated an exercise of personal arm-twisting on the holdout bankers, who were duly identified in the national media. He devised a standby emergency plan as a last resort, telling the die-hards that their failure to assent would trigger notice to President Carter that chapter eleven bankruptcy petitions would be filed, imperiling the repayment prospects of all existing lenders. It was Iacocca-type muscle at its crunchiest—"hardball," he could call it—and it worked when one of the last intransigents signed the loan package, American Bank and Trust of Rockford, Illinois, near Chrysler's Omni-Horizon plant in Belvidere and a $525,000 Chrysler creditor.

Once again, as with the reluctant Congress, the weather-beaten U.S. bank community undoubtedly never would have doubled their loans to the distressed Chrysler—federal guarantees or not—had it not been for the presence of Iacocca and the show of his mystique and that of his corporate disciples. Greenwald and the missionary Steve Miller, who tirelessly scoured the nation to pursue the bankers, infused the creditors with their leader's zeal. Meeting after meeting was held, one involving twenty-five chief executive officers of leading Chrysler banks, building up the inevitable assent by acclamation.

It was another one of those unattainable peaks that only an Iacocca-led juggernaut could ascend. The final 100 percent approval by all four hundred-plus banks was announced by Miller on April 17. The Treasury Department then insisted that the banks accept a stock equity in Chrysler in exchange for delayed interest payments.

At the end of the tortuous trail, though Chrysler had failed to sell $300 million worth of additional assets as required by the loan guarantee act, and despite last-minute objections from a handful of banks, the trailblazing bailout was assured. It had taken Steve Miller no fewer than 117 airplane fights to see realization of the goal: Drawdown by Chrysler of the first $500 million of federally guaranteed loans on June 24, 1980. Chrysler had its lease on life, and Iacocca could concentrate on what he did best— promoting an "all-new" line of cars.

"It's easy for a company boss," says a veteran management consultant, "to run things when business is good and the economy is strong. It's much more difficult when the economy is slowing down and business is lousy. It's sheer hell—even for an Iacocca, I would guess—when your company is a basket case and the wolf is at the door."

Iacocca speaks of sleepless nights during the

1979–80 years as he battled to save Chrysler. The market share was flirting with the low-end 8 percent range, prompting the usually self-assured Iacocca to admit, "I was losing my ass out there, and it was a new experience."

It became fashionable to lampoon the impoverished Chrysler. TV comic Johnny Carson drew laughs when he characterized a "mean" type as one who would call up Chrysler to ask, "How's business?" The cartoonists likened Chrysler to a big lady. It didn't help Iacocca's personal or mental health, in the midst of all this travail, when he suffered a vertigo attack on one of his frequent visits to Congress. "All the tension and pressure made me feel like I had rocks in my head," he said. "But somehow I muddled through."

One of the toughest tasks undertaken by Iacocca, in the dark days of early 1980, was to pare Chrysler's white-collar ranks by some 7000 persons. Only a few months earlier, 8500 salaried-workers had been decked, adding up to total annual savings of approximately $500 million.

Though chief executive officers rarely if ever put themselves through this type of ordeal, Iacocca decided to fire most of the senior staffers himself. He thought that his own ouster by Henry Ford II had prepared him for the job, but it turned out otherwise. More of the dischargees than he imagined argued with him, cried, asked for reconsideration, or threatened to sue.

Iacocca tried to be generous with early-retirement settlements and pensions. Strict rules on longevity or age were bent at his dictate, more often than not. Still, Iacocca found the exercise especially difficult because so many of Chrysler's past mistakes had been committed by top management and most of the underlings, however advanced in compensation or position, were merely carrying out orders. "Watching people get kicked around had a big impact on me," said Iacocca. "It make me think a lot more about social responsibility, a lesson I never learned at Ford. There, like the rest of top management, I was above it all. Also, we never had a crisis of this magnitude. In the past, I never had to do much laying off."

The end result of all the pruning done on the Chrysler oak by Iacocca was to excise the "staff" managers and elevate the responsibility of the "line" officials who at Ford and to some extent at Chrysler took their marching orders from "staff." Iacocca had taken a dim view of "staff experts" back at Ford, needling them as "Harvard Business School graduates who may not know their asses from their elbows." He preferred experience and tenure over sheer advanced education or Ivy League credentials.

To Iacocca, nothing is more irksome than the conflict engendered by a superior "who's never run anything" finding fault with a thirty-year staffer. He doesn't rule out a staff setup "in moderation," but

Chrysler's overriding need was for car and truck producers and marketers. Thus, out of necessity, Chrysler evolved into a leaner management organization in relation to its volume than GM or Ford. Even Maestro Iacocca, coming from a top-heavy orchestra at Ford, found it easier to run the assemblage with fewer hands. The outcome didn't assuage the pain of firing so many veterans at Chrysler, but Iacocca rejoiced in the fact that the end justified the means—a reflection of the fact that he can be cold-blooded when he believes the greater good is being served.

In other words, Iacocca can be rough and tough when things don't go his way or when subordinates foul up. Sometimes his acerbic handling of underlings borders on the needlessly vindictive, as a vice-president of thirty years' seniority with Chrysler recalled after being poleaxed in Iacocca's office in 1980.

"He told me a month earlier how he liked my work on the future products," the victim said. "I was getting along well with Hal Sperlich, and we were weaving together the major features of the K-cars, Laser and Daytona sports coupes, and mini-vans—all the vehicles which really got Chrysler rolling.

"I knew things were too good to last because of all my fellow officers from the old Chrysler days who were getting pink slips. He called me in, found some trifling excuse to chew me out, and then lowered the boom.

"He said a 'new' team had to be put together, now that the feds were overseeing the company with their loan guarantees. They gave me a good early-out settlement, but he made me feel like shit. I should have sued them, but I wound up with a good job at one of Chrysler's key suppliers and slowly the wound healed.

"But a lot of the so-called Iacocca mystique is sheer intimidation when it comes to dealing with even the highest-ranking executives. It worked at Chrysler, fortunately, but a lot of good people were hurt by the guy."

Iacocca's best-selling autobiography, of course, glosses over this aspect of his character. Many present-day critics reject his argument that his later rancor toward longtime Chryslerites was "justified" by his own treatment at the hands of Henry Ford II. His older daughter Kathi, who early in 1985 was appointed head of a special foundation by her father to dispense profits from the autobiography, was asked about this and replied, "Anyone who expects him to forgive Ford for what he did to us doesn't know my father."

The K-car launch in the fall of 1980 was almost torpedoed by one of Iacocca's first product mistakes. He sided with the Greenwald-led finance staff in opting for a "rich" mix of factory-installed options on the first Dodge Aries and Plymouth Reliant cars reaching dealers, thereby hoping to bring in some sorely needed cash fast. The newly constituted Chrysler Loan Guarantee Board was breathing down Iacocca's neck, and he felt the boxy front-wheel-drive compacts were sound enough to justify loading the early models with automatic transmissions, power steering, fancy radios, and other options. Typically, Iacocca's sales staff had cajoled the dealers to order a bountiful supply of 1981 models, though they little expected that the vast majority would be priced at the upper end of the range instead of at the lower levels as advertised.

By November, dealer orders for the K-cars backed up as disappointed shoppers complained about nearly five-figure delivered prices far above the $7000-ish base prices promised in the Iacocca-signed ads. To add to the marketing snafu, production workers encountered problems with the new automated equipment at the Chrysler Jefferson plant in Detroit, delaying production just as the introductory ads were at a crescendo.

To make matters worse, interest rates on loans began heading "north," and Chrysler's hopes for a tidy fourth-quarter profit vanished. Iacocca exhibited his expertise as a generalist by devising a unique "floating" interest rebate that guaranteed every installment loan buyer the difference between the going rate and the 13 percent rate at which the 1981-model season had begun.

The production snags eventually were resolved,

but a scapegoat had to be found, and one was: Chrysler holdover Dick Vining, whom Iacocca had promoted to executive vice-president for engineering and manufacturing. Iacocca replaced him not with a Ford alumnus but with the frequently bypassed Chrylser production ace, Steve Sharf, who had brought into being the trouble-free and economical 2.2-liter four-cylinder engine that powered the K-cars.

The relatively high-quality K-body cars notwithstanding, Chrysler still was grappling with cash problems toward the end of 1980. President Carter had been soundly drubbed in his bid for reelection by a free-enterprise zealot, Ronald Reagan, who was no enthusiast for federal bailouts of privately owned corporations, to say the least.

Worse, the K-car launch mess and the sky-high interest rates had cleaned the till of the first $800 million drawn by Chrysler against the guaranteed loan total. Chrysler was as impoverished at Christmas 1980 as it had been the year before.

Outgoing Treasury Secretary Miller, now also head of the Chrysler Loan Guarantee Board, called for new concessions by those in the Chrysler community—even after Iacocca concocted a new assortment of contributions from the workers, suppliers, and banks. These would be in addition to a further draw from the loan guarantees.

Miller's stance left Iacocca with little choice, though he constantly bristled at the intrusions of the loan board."For each drawdown," Iacocca groaned, "we had to face up to the bad headlines. It was terrible. Each time we went back for more money, our sales dropped off."

On January 19,1981, the day before the inauguration of President Reagan, Miller presided over the last meeting of the Carter administration's Chrysler Loan Guarantee Board. Iacocca accepted an additional $400 million in new loans, raising the total to a cool $1.2 billion and leaving $300 million for a last-ditch draw if needed (it never was). The UAW agreed to a third wave of concessions and gave Chrysler an aggregate edge of nearly $1 billion in labor costs over a three-year period against Ford and GM. Chrysler was all but freed of nonfederal-guarantee debt as the result of all the machinations. The while-collar force was cut—again.

By the spring of 1981, Iacocca was presiding over a Chrysler as "lean and mean" as it had ever been. The non-North American subsidiaries, the dealership real-estate unit, Dodge Main, even the corporate airplanes were things of the past. But bankruptcy had been averted. The Loan Guarantee Act, designed solely to preserve Chrysler, had done so and in the process had blazed a trail that could be traveled again some day.

As Iacocca looked to the future, perhaps sensing that he had turned the corner and could go nowhere but up, he could take pride in the fact that the products he was brewing in Chrylser's vats were the best in thirty years, that the often-angry workers were knocking themselves out to improve efficiency, that the money crunch was history, that Chrysler finally had its act together, and that the son of immigrants from Italy had brought a major automaker back from the graveyard—as none other than nemesis Henry Ford II had thirty-five years before!

16

FROM K-DAY

TO HEYDAY

THE K-CAR CAME TO BE LEE IACOCCA'S SPRING-board to success at Chrysler, just as the Mustang had brought him to the pinnacle at Ford. From K-Day on, once the initial launch glitches had been overcome, Iacocca piloted the Chrysler spaceship on a spectacular ascent.

There were adverse periods along the way, highlighted by a jarring passenger-car sales decline of 20.8 percent in the deep industry recession year of 1982. But by that time the K-car compacts were firmly placed on the U.S. market, and the surge of derivative models was arriving from Chrysler with such marketing success that 1983 brought a whopping 51.2 percent climb in new-car sales and 1984 a 37.4 percent jump from 1983, aside from the truck boom (generated by the K-body-spawned minivans) that started in 1984.

"The smart guys," Iacocca declares, "use interchangeable parts to get their costs down. That's not only permissible, it's also essential. These days, to do a new car from scratch when you're unsure of the volume is a sure formula for bankruptcy."

Iacocca had avoided the "sure formula" before Chrysler won its federal bailout, and he steered clear of rocky shores thereafter with his cost-minded adherence to the K-car as the root of Chrysler's future products. It might not have worked, though, without the marketing brainstorms that Iacocca and his ad "guys" conceived to convince buyers that they were getting markedly different vehicles from the plain jane Reliant and Aries boxcars that had triggered Chrysler's recovery.

And in truth, the promotional drives might have foundered had Iacocca been less of a risk-taker and more of a doctrinaire business "manager." Says Warren Bennis, an Iacocca-type "leader"—even in the kind of crunch period gripping Chrysler *after* arrival of the K-cars—still might not have been "paying enough attention to doing the right thing, while paying too much attention to doing things right."

Chrysler, having wound up 1980 with a new loss of $1.7 billion, still was mired deep in quicksand even with the K-cars on the market. Ford had lost $1.5 billion in the same year, lacking a front-wheel drive compact to rival Chrysler's K-cars and GM's X-cars, and the gutsy Iacocca asked an assistant, Tom Denomme, to work up a formal proposal for a Chrysler-Ford merger!

"For Ford," Iacocca believed, "a merger with Chrysler represented the fastest, easiest way to get back to their original position of being a strong number two. . . . If a merger with Chrysler went through, Ford would have been at 75 percent of GM's strength in U.S. car sales. Then we would have seen a real horse race."

We also would have seen Iacocca's retirement from the auto industry, because the then new chairman of Ford, Philip Caldwell, understandably couldn't have divided authority with the former Ford president. Yet though the merger idea was doomed to stay grounded after a terse rejection by Ford directors, the grandiose nature of the plan typified the innovativeness of Iacocca's managerial approach. It would be hard to imagine a Chairman Caldwell at Chrysler proposing the same consolidation to a Chairman Iacocca at Ford, personality conflicts aside.

By the time Chrysler got its 1981-model K-cars untracked from their launch problems, it was time for 1982 models and for another cash crisis; this would be the last one tackled by Iacocca. As of November 1, 1981, Chrysler counted a grand total of $1 million in its payroll account. For a business that spent close to $50 million a day, that was like petty cash to Iacocca.

But after the agonies of the preceding years, it was no time to call it quits and head for Federal Bankruptcy Court. Iacocca, declaring "we had to be magicians," juggled payables here and pleaded for suppliers to extend credit terms there. By now it seemed like old hat, but it worked. The upshot was that Chrysler never missed a payroll or a supplier payment, however late.

There was an element of fear on the part of creditors and suppliers in the rescue of Chrysler, of course. Who wanted to be the SOB to push Chrysler into involuntary bankruptcy, and what good would it have done the unpaid petitioner to do so in any event? Iacocca could be a consummate opportunist when it came to exploiting that fear, and more than one supplier who felt enough was enough in the slow-pay Chrysler account shrank from precipitate litigation against Chrysler at the last minute for fear of Iacocca's wrath.

What the constant attention to Chrysler's peaks and valleys amassed for Iacocca himself was exposure—of a kind almost unparalleled in U.S. corporate history. The names John F. Welch, Jr., R. Gordon McGovern, and Roberto C. Goizueta mean next to nothing to the American public at large in spite of the fact that they are hard-charging chairmen in the Iacocca vein of three of the largest consumer product manufacturers—General Electric,

Campbell Soup, and Coca-Cola, respectively. Each has set out to streamline and invigorate a phlegmatic organization, though fortunately without the near-terminal malady that plagued Chrysler. Yet as insiders who wouldn't dream of appearing in TV ads or leading crusades against national trade policies, none of the top executives of GE, Campbell Soup, or Coca-Cola enjoys the reputation of Iacocca.

Even Iacocca, perhaps envincing a bit of false modesty, says he was also "convinced that any corporate chairman who appears in his company's ads has got to be on an ego trip. Whenever I've seen a CEO pushing his own company, it's left a bad taste in my mouth."

Iacocca overcame the "bad taste" syndrome in star-quality fashion, or he would have been laughed off the tube early on. There was an element of lucky timing in his commercials because the master actor himself, Ronald Reagan, was communicating from the White House from 1981 on and the audience was growing inured to superhype at the highest level.

When Chrysler's marketing executives and advertising agencies first proposed to Iacocca that he personally pitch the company's products and "institutional" attributes on selected TV spots and print ads, the chairman was decidedly not averse. He had never done this at Ford, although he was one of the auto industry's most forceful speakers and was more knowledgeable about effective salesmanship than most corporate chairman or presidents in any industry.

It was in 1981 and 1982, when Chrysler was staggering and almost terminal, that Iacocca's direct-approach ads began in earnest. Many doubted that the Iacocca spots would help business much, pointing to the comparable effort of former astronaut Frank Borman as chairman of Eastern Airlines.

But Iacocca proved the detractors wrong. He attained the celebrity status of TV's Dan Rather or Phil Donahue. Chrysler sales rose steadily as more and more Iacocca spots appeared on prime-time dramas, during major athletic events, and between segments of the morning news shows. Chrysler surveys showed that new-car buyers who had ducked Chrysler products for years or had never visited a Chrysler showroom became "converts" as a result of the "credibility"—an almost undefinable quality—embodied in Iacocca's assertion, "If You Can Find a Better Car, Buy One."

The messages were upbeat and blunt, pitching the products and the company, rapping the competition, daring the viewers or readers to visit Chrysler dealerships and compare them against GM or Ford.

Chrysler might have made it without the Iacocca commercials, even after the initial major mistake with the new front-wheel-drive K-body cars in the fall of 1980. But a surprisingly large number of Chrysler product buyers for the K-body car and its

derivative later models—the E-cars and the rest—
said it was belief in Iacocca's message and sincerity
that motivated their purchase. He backed up the
ads in person, not through a Ricardo Montalban or
Ed McMahon. It was a risky undertaking for an
American industrial captain.

It's safe to say, looking back over eighty years of
American automotive history, that no other senior
executive could have accomplished the Iacocca feat
of resurrecting the sales volume of a line of cars
that such a preponderant majority of Americans had
written off as defunct. Cars (and trucks) are too
essential to the life-style of Americans for them to
risk a heavy investment in "a set of wheels" with a
reputation for poor quality such as Chrysler, Dodge,
and Plymouth held by 1980. "Let the losers go" had
been the auto industry's modus operandi. It would
have been unthinkable for Henry Ford II to beg for
Edsel or Pinto sales—or for GM's then-Chairman
Fred Donner to plead for the TV public to buy Chevrolet Corvairs when Ralph Nader went after the
"unsafe" rear-engine cars twenty years ago.

Iacocca would be the first to admit that he might
have flopped as a TV hustler without decent new
products to replace the aging and unwanted Chrysler fleet of the 1970s. Chrysler's pre-Iacocca decision to switch to lighter-weight front-wheel-drive
cars, starting with the entry-level Plymouth Horizon
and Dodge Omni subcompacts, gave Iacocca the
ammunition, he needed to reassert the company's

competitiveness. Thus, timing benefited the Iacocca message as the worst auto sales recession since the 1930s heightened public interest in lighter-weight front-driven products. The Omni and Horizon were introduced in 1978 just as Iacocca was coming to Chrysler, and they were the first subcompacts built in the United States by that company, in spite of the fact that GM and Ford had been offering domestic subcompacts since 1959. Chrysler's outmoded rear-wheel-drive compacts—its bread-and-butter Plymouth Volare and Dodge Aspen cars—would not be replaced by the trendier Plymouth Reliant and Dodge Aries until 1981, when Iacocca decided that it was not only timely but also crucial that he go to bat in person for the sinking ship.

Actually, Iacocca's first and in some ways hardest challenge as a first-person company salesman was not the public but the long-suffering Chrysler-Plymouth and Dodge dealer organizations. Dealer attrition had struck Chrysler in many key markets even before he got to the Highland Park headquarters; Iacocca explained later that "for years the company had been shipping them junk and expecting them to sell it." Disenchanted dealers, tempted by the franchise appeals of Japanese importers, could not be expected to hang in there while any bailout chairman or president pleaded for John Q. Public to "think Chrysler."

Iacocca made "must" appearances at dealer meetings, as well as at conventions of state and national dealer associations. His Ford training, starting back in Allentown as a truck zone manager, had equipped him for dealer contact unlike the finance or manufacturing types who had run Chrysler previously or who were in charge at the competition. He was at ease with "dealer talk" and responded to dealer suggestions with a receptiveness never experienced by the company's retailers in the regimes headed by Chairman Riccardo and Townsend. Chrysler's revival hinged on strong dealers in key markets—a fact that Iacocca valued even as he masterminded the financial rescue of Chrysler and the revitalization of the product lines to embrace medium-size cars, sporty coupes, and pioneering minivans. To paraphrase an Iacocca axiom, "The symbols (products) mean nothing if the values (dealers) aren't there."

From the recession-induced nadir of Chrysler new-car sales in 1982, it was relatively smooth sailing upward for the Iacocca team. The Bergmoser, Matthias, and Laux trio were winding down, and Laux was replaced as sales executive vice-president by former Ford and Chrysler sales and marketing officer John Naughton, who had an acquaintance with literally hundreds of Chrysler dealers. Naughton himself fell victim to an Iacocca "shocker" in 1983 when Bennett E. Bidwell, a former Ford sales vice-president, regarded as one of the savviest marketing men in the auto industry, resigned as president of Hertz to join Chrysler as executive vice-president for sales and marketing. The move seated Bidwell on Chrysler's new four-man "office of the chairman" with Iacocca, Vice-Chairman Greenwald, and President Sperlich—but it infuriated the crusty Naughton, whom Iacocca had not informed of his shakeup.

The callous Bidwell-for-Naughton shift reflected a flaw in Iacocca's personality, to be sure, although Bidwell fitted more smoothly into the Iacocca team than Naughton, a more conservative marketing official. Iacocca, embarrassed by the incident, makes no mention in his autobiography of Naughton's stint at Chrysler, during which many key dealers on the verge of dumping Dodge or Chrysler-Plymouth were prevailed on to "hang in there."

As Chrysler has prospered, several other defects in Iacocca's managerial personality surfaced. He is devoted to his two daughters, and his wife Mary's death in 1983, at the age of fifty-seven, left a deep blow. Yet none of Chrysler's thirty officers is female, unlike GM and Ford, because Iacocca often seems uncomfortable relating to women in professional capacities such as manufacturing or marketing.

Iacocca can be inconsistent, for all his missionary causes. He ordered Chrysler to sue the GM-Toyota joint venture to build cars in California, a public relations ploy he abandoned in April 1985 when Chrysler decided to pursue its own U.S. assembly joint venture with Mitsubishi. He is sometimes manic about ideas, waking underlings up in the middle of the night or on weekends and ordering revisions after revisions.

"Never contradict him in a meeting of more than three or four people," confides an upper-level Chrysler staffer, "even if his facts are dead wrong. Wait until you see him one on one, or two on one, or his pride will eat you up alive."

Iacocca can be oversimplistic. This might be a plus if your message is selling Dodge Daytonas. But the following statement from his autobiography reads like third-grade prose: "Since Eisenhower, we haven't found ourselves a leader we can depend on. Kennedy got killed. Johnson dragged us into a war. Nixon disgraced us. Ford was an appointed interim leader. Carter, for all his virtues, turned out wrong for his time. Reagan lives in the past."

If such tomtom beats as this diminish the reputation of the speaker as a clairvoyant pundit, they do serve to enhance Iacocca's tendency to favor style over substance on many issues. And style counts more and more these days, linked as it is to success vis-à-vis failure. In the last three years of the Iacocca-led Chrysler, another axiom endorsed by most Americans rang truer than ever: "Nothing succeeds like success—and nothing fails like failure."

By late 1982, as the 1983-model season arrived and with it higher-profit upscale versions of the basic K-cars, Chrysler showed its first fourth-quarter net profit in five years. An automotive sales upturn was underway, pushing Chrysler to a $170 million profit for calendar 1982 and an all-time company record of $701 million in 1983. After net losses amounting to $3.5 billion from 1978 (when Iacocca joined the company) through 1981, there was no doubt that the Chrysler recovery and the Iacocca era were now inseparably linked.

By way of celebrating the turnaround, which rocketed the price of Chrysler common stock from a low of $3 a share tenfold to the low thirties (it reached $37 the week of April 15, 1985), Iacocca sold a $432 million offering of Chrysler stock in the spring of 1983 and then made a typically unexpected decision: To get the feds off his back and dispose of those high-interest-rate guaranteed loans, Chrysler would pay back the *full* shot of $1.2 billion—*seven years* ahead of the 1990 due date.

Rejecting the cautious recommendations of some senior executives, Iacocca asserted that he was upbeat enough about the company's future to forgo the loan cushion.

In reality, the chairman was fed up with the ministrations of the loan board, now led by an unsupportive Donald Regan as President Reagan's Treasury Secretary. The board maintained a liaison office in Chrysler's Highland Park headquarters and was more of a hindrance than a help to the self-assured Iacocca. Too, Iacocca saw full repayment as another public relations bonanza. And it did clear Chrysler's ledger of 15 percent-plus interest charges on the largest chunk of the guaranteed loans at a time when interest rates were heading "south" at a rapid clip.

In the end, however, in what some political analysts interpret as a partial rebuff because of Iacocca's growing ties with the Democrats, Regan insisted on extracting every penny of profit for the Treasury from the 14.4 million Chrysler warrants that the loan board had collected back in 1980—at a mere $13 a share of Chrysler stock.

Iacocca's demand that the warrants be surrendered, on the ground that Chrysler already had paid astronomical costs for the guaranteed loans ($404 million in interest, $33 million in administrative fees, another $67 million to attorneys and investment firms) met with a flat turndown. Chrysler stock was selling in mid-1983 for $30 a share, and the profit was too bountiful for Regan to dismiss.

"Everyone thought we were being greedy," Iacocca avers in a rare concession of error. "From a public-relations standpoint, it was a disaster. One minute we were heroes for paying back our loans early. The next thing we knew, we were bums. It was a painful experience."

The government turned down Chrysler's offers of first $120 million, then $187 million, and finally $250 million for the warrants. Regan wanted the full profit of upward of $300 million at Chrysler's stock price at the time. Chrysler wound up buying back the warrants as top bidder at an "auction" for $311 million, despite Iacocca's personal appeals to

President Reagan. Iacocca is irate over what he believes to be Regan's desire to "screw Chrysler—let's get every cent we can."

The incident displays Iacocca's steel will and go-for-broke inclinations, qualities that probably could have used a bit of tempering in view of the fact that he was chastising a powerful Cabinet member who eventually became White House Chief of Staff. Iacocca lashed out at Regan at the time as a subordinate disobeying his boss, declaring that "where I come from, if I as a CEO tell someone to do something and I never get an answer back, I fire him. It's incredible that this guy Regan could sit out this guy Reagan." Lese majesty—and in writing!

There's no need to worry, however. Iacocca's Chrysler rolled with the punch and escalated its net sales and net profits in 1984 to new records again—$19,573,000,000 and $2,380,000,000, respectively. The march of new front-wheel-drive cars continued with the introduction of two sporty upscale sedans for the 1985 model year, also derived from the K-body cars; the Chrysler LeBaron GTS and the Dodge Lancer. Chrysler agreed with its Japanese partner, Mitsubishi, to build small cars in the United States as a joint-venture assembly plant in the Midwest.

And the board of directors rewarded Iacocca handsomely on June 6, 1985, as Chrysler reached a sixtieth birthday that few thought several years before ever would come to pass. Iacocca's salary in 1984 had been raised to $569,838, from $475,308 in 1983. He picked up a 1983 bonus of $625,000. He exercised stock options that produced a paper profit of $4.32 million and stood to add between $5 million and $10 million in May 1985 with exercise of options on another 448,000 shares of Chrysler stock. All told, Iacocca scooped up 1984 earnings in the range of $13 million.

In addition, a 1985 bonus was to be granted, and he would receive the following stock gifts and options: 150,000 shares of Chrysler stock if he is employed there November 2, 1986; 50,000 shares if employed December 8, 1987, plus options for 200,000 shares at $27.94 a share.

The 1984 achievements for Chrysler added to Iacocca's luster as a haloed rescuer almost without parallel in American business industry. No corporation so broke and desperate had ever managed such a spectacular upward leap. The personal rewards under the American free-enterprise system were there for the taking, and Iacocca was ready to share in the hard-won fruits of the Chrysler turnaround along with his colleagues.

On May 17, 1985, Iacocca presided over the annual meeting of Chrysler shareholders at Anaheim, California, where a special tour of Chrysler's new Shelby "performance center" on high-tech cars was offered. The *real* performance center was centered in Iacocca's office in Highland Park, Michigan, base of a corporate chief becoming a legend in his time.

17

HOW TO BECOME
A HERO

A MERICANS LIKE THEIR HEROES—ATH-
letic, military, literary, showbiz, even corporate. Heroes in the business category,
however, are few and far between by contrast with the Babe Ruths, Dwight Eisenhowers,
Ernest Hemingways, Katharine Hepburns, and John
F. Kennedys. Alfred P. Sloan, Jr., indisputably the
creator of today's General Motors structure, was not
the "hero type" and preferred for the most part to
operate within corporate boardrooms rather than in
the public domain. Only Henry Ford and his grand-
son, Henry Ford II, became automotive executive
role models whom many outsiders could recognize
or admire. No senior officer of Chrysler until Iacocca,

nor of GM to this day, including the communications-minded present chairman, Roger B. Smith, achieved a celebrity's reputation even though "giant GM" in 1984 rolled up an astounding $83.9 billion in sales and revenues and a record $4.5 billion in net profit.

How, then, did Iacocca become a folk legend in his time? Many other moribund corporations have been raised from the ashes, Phoenix-style, or built from scratch into giant complexes with faultless blue-chip reputations. But except for a smattering of corporate historians and financial analysts, who recalls the first chairmen of Texaco or IBM? Iacocca became what *Fortune* magazine described as "the most famous and most popular American businessman." What were the ingredients that this son of Italian immigrants employed to reach such a status?

Effective use of communications and public relations certainly was the yeast of the "heroics" recipe used by Iacocca at Chrysler. It didn't hurt the imagery that Chrysler, the nation's number-three auto and truck builder, was down and nearly out—the better to be resuscitated. A losing cause turned into a big winner always holds magnetic appeal for the public at large, investing the miracle worker with cosmic power. If Roger Smith or Ford's present chairman, Donald F. Petersen, had taken the Chrysler challenge and turned the dying company around, there would have been applause and admiration, but nothing like the hero worship that trails Iacocca.

It was Lee's achievement, not wholly unintended, to don a halo while at the same time reviving Chrysler.

Getting fired by Henry Ford II, before the Chrysler chapters in his life story, advanced the hero-molding process, but it by no means assured its success. Henry the Deuce and Iacocca himself had booted or let go a dozen or more highly touted senior Ford executives over a thirty-five-year span. Many went on to leadership positions at a number of estimable organizations—Bell and Howell, Firestone, the World Bank, White Motor Company, and Stanford University Business School. But heroes they did not become; they survived their purge from Ford's Dearborn headquarters with few lasting scars.

Of course, none of the previous Ford employees wrote a book about his rise and fall and rise, choosing not to tell tales out of school. But Iacocca's best-selling autobiography, it is fair to conclude, attained commercial credibility *after* the fact of his successful resuscitation of Chrysler. The Iacocca memoir shared a "true confessions" kind of appeal with the popular saga of fired GM executive John Z. DeLorean, *On a Clear Day You Can See General Motors*, written by J. Patrick Wright in an as-told-to format. Both revealed inner corporate workings and personal horror stories of keen interest to those as eager to see top executives humbled as to find new victims with which to identify.

But anyone looking for 100 percent objectivity in

either the Iacocca or the DeLorean book would be hard put to find it. DeLorean, who after his exit from GM departed from Iacocca's career track with a new enterprise, confined his memoirs to a one-sided account of what GM had done to him. To the surprise of many automotive associates, so did Iacocca omit from his autobiography any effort to tell both sides of his story. After all, Iacocca was a highly recognized and wildly successful figure when his book appeared in 1984—yet he too displayed an overriding ego bordering on self-righteousness.

It was this show of ego in the years at Chrysler that lies at the heart of the answer to the question, "How did he become a corporate superstar?" A self-effacing executive, shrewd in finance or marketing, might have turned Chrysler from a devastating loser into a big winner, but he would never have emerged as a cynosure attracting an average of five hundred letters and invitations a day. Fan mail doesn't flow to Roger Smith or perhaps even to Don Petersen in that volume—even though GM and Ford are far bigger companies with far more vehicle owners, shareholders, and employees.

"Iacocca's fame has done great good for Chrysler products," says James Tolley, vice-president of public affairs for Chrysler. This worked the other way, too, in that Iacocca made use of Chrysler products and the company's rise from rags to riches as propellants for his ascent to stardom. The driver needed the vehicle as much as the vehicle needed the driver, and both benefited accordingly.

Having been burned by another automotive superstar, Henry Ford II, Iacocca entered his Chrysler period with few illusions about the trustworthiness or real-world influence of top executives, political leaders, or popular heroes. He had seen too many idols with feet of clay. But the Chrysler rescue operation that he so brilliantly directed made him into one of those heroes, whether he intended it to be so or not, and showed at the same time how a top executive can use communications to serve both his company and himself.

Is it, however, sound corporate policy for the chairman of the board to become so deeply embroiled in a public issue that *USA Today* can headline a front-page story, "Iacocca vs. Reagan on car quotas"?

Or should prudent outside directors opt to blow the whistle on such confrontations with the U.S. President in the time-tested belief that it doesn't pay to fight city hall for any company, much less the number-three automaker in a fiercely competitive industry?

Lee Iacocca has marched to his own drummer on policy matters about which he feels strongly. He has squared off time and again against President Reagan and many of Reagan's Cabinet officers and policy administrators. With candor that is as natural for Iacocca as a lion's roar, he has debated the

Reaganites on Japan's "voluntary" new-car export quotas to the United States, on the growing federal budget deficit, on the lack of a national energy policy, on the "hypocrisy" of both Republicans and Democrats who fought a federal loan guarantee act for Chrysler while voting for loan bailouts for New York City, Penn Central, and Lockheed, and supporting farm and veterans' subsidies.

Not a few corporation watchers, and reportedly a handful of outside Chrysler directors, have questioned the long-range value to Chrysler of Iacocca's constant confrontations. "Lee is Lee, and there's no denying he makes headlines as a champion and a disputant," said one outside Chrysler director who insisted on anonymity. "But sometimes I wonder if Chrysler's best interest is served by the chairman's feuding in the media against a President who was elected twice with huge majorities. I'm not convinced that any corporate leader should tackle the national administration with such fervor. They have the power to really hurt us."

As the March 31, 1985, deadline approached for determination of whether the Japanese quotas should be renewed for a fifth year, Iacocca and his vice-chairman, Gerald Greenwald, spearheaded the auto industry's campaign to preserve the quotas in the face of clear signals from the White House that Reagan had decided not to seek new restraints. Greenwald warned that phaseout of the quotas, which limited imports of Japanese-built cars to

1,850,000 units in the 1984–85 year, could result in such an escalation of shipments from Japan that up to 750,000 American jobs could be lost.

Iacocca issued what many analysts interpreted as a threat to go offshore with Chrysler's small-car production if the quotas were to cease. He bluntly said Chrysler would have to reconsider whether to build its restyled subcompact cars, the P-body replacements for the aging Dodge Omni and Plymouth Horizon, at Belvidere, Illinois, or in the Far East or Mexico. The quotas were increased 24.3 percent for 1984–86 at the behest of the Japanese government, spurring Iacocca to shift the P-cars from Belvidere to Chrysler's newer plant at Sterling Heights, Michigan.

The battle over quotas, while an issue of utmost importance to Chrysler and all domestic automakers, still rubbed the White House in an abrasive way, reviving the fact that Iacocca had been proposed as a Democratic presidential nominee in 1984 and was briefly considered by Walter Mondale as a vice-presidential running mate. (Iacocca constantly denies political ambitions and was not a serious contender for the second spot on the Democratic ticket, although several secret polls taken before former U.S. Representative Geraldine Ferraro's selection gave Iacocca a surprisingly high percentage.)

Chrysler's leadership was joined by executives at Ford and American Motors in advocating continuation of quotas. General Motors, seeking to import more small cars from its Japanese partners, Isuzu and Suzuki, urged that the quotas be dumped or raised substantially. But it was the flamboyant Iacocca who became identified as the foremost proponent of the quotas, for better or worse.

Conversion of the quota issue to a personality clash—"Iacocca vs. Reagan"—held multiple dangers for the company at whose helm Iacocca stood. Washington insiders reported that Reagan was so piqued at the flinty Chrysler chairman for "flirting" with Mondale and chastising Reagan on federal budget deficits that he was leaning toward scrapping the quotas out of revenge as much as out of philosophical belief in free trade. In other words, Iacocca was to blame for any dire consequences after the end of the ceilings on Japanese imports.

Ad hominem prejudices are at the root of many policy decisions, but Chrysler's chief executive officer may wind up with mud on his face and problems for his company as a result of his pugnacious overreach against a President with such dedicated beliefs and such an overwhelming following. The forum of the podium of a major consumer product company helped Iacocca become a national celebrity but may not prove the best launching pad for political crusades.

Iacocca also has refrained from mincing words even when his acid spills over onto Chrysler's own "captive" automaking supplier, Mitsubishi. The Mitsubishi-assembled Colt subcompact cars have over the past fifteen years been the source of considerable sales and profits for Chrysler and its dealers—proving a windfall in many lean times when Chrysler either lacked small cars of its own or was encountering stormy sales weather. The Japanese automaker has organized its own importing organization in the United States but has provided Conquest sports coupes, small pickup trucks, and unique seven-seat Vista station wagons to the Chrysler import lineup. In addition, Chrysler has asked Mitsubishi to develop a small and sorely needed V-6 engine to offer seekers of greater horsepower a competitive option on Chrysler's bread-and-butter front-wheel-drive compact and mid-size cars.

Nevertheless, in April 1984, Iacocca gave *U.S. News & World Report* an interview in which he bashed the trade advantages of Japan over the United States. The portions of this interview dealing with the "Japan issue" reveal more than the rhetoric of a mindless domestic automaker railing at tough competition from abroad, however. Iacocca demonstrates an interview style which is at the same time hard-hitting and quite persuasive:

A. We have got to decide what free and fair trade is all about, and we've got to try to level the playing field—to be competitive. These are the gut issues.

It's not understood well by people, but by 1985, having invested as an industry some 80 billion dollars, we will have gotten pretty competitive. Our own 700-million-dollar plant in Windsor [Ontario] that makes the T-115 minivans is so state-of-the-art that the Japanese are coming to visit it with their cameras so that can imitate us.

We've still got a rock around our neck of about $600 a car in costs to control—made up half of higher labor rates than the Japanese pay their workers, and about half of inefficiencies that are built into our system. Much of the difference in labor rates, by the way, comes from runaway health costs, which by themselves come to $600 a car.

As for inefficiencies, there are problems with work rules, white-collar productivity, lousy plant layouts, poor floor of materials—call it stupid management, if you want.

Q. If you're so close to being competitive with the Japanese, then what's the cause for concern?

A. My great fear is that I'll invest all this money and work with the UAW to control costs even more, and still be $1,500 a car out of whack with the Japanese.

Q. Why?

A. Because we're talking about political issues

over which I as a businessman have no control. Take the exchange rate of the yen. There isn't one expert in the world who wouldn't argue that the yen is undervalued against the dollar. Translated into the price of a Toyota vs. a Chrysler, that's a $1,000 yoke we carry.

Now, we're told that the undervaluation is caused by the strength of the dollar, and that the dollar is held up by high interest rates. But the exchange rate has stayed at 230 yen while U.S. interest rates have gone from 10 to 22 percent, back to 10 percent and then up again. The Japanese are manipulating the yen to keep it undervalued. [Note: The exchange rate had risen to about 260 yen to the dollar in late February 1985.]

Our other disadvantage against the Japanese is that we pay our government income taxes and they pay their government value-added taxes—except that their value-added tax is refunded if the car is exported.

So the same Toyota might cost the Tokyo housewife $9,000 but the San Francisco housewife only $8,000—another clip against us.

Why do I spend so much time in Washington? It's not to be a good citizen or to mouth off. Finally you realize that unless you start to attack some of these root problems, you're never going to have a world-class U.S. auto industry.

Q. What should the U.S. do about trade with Japan?

A. This administration and Congress are going into 1984 with two scandalous marks on their report cards—a 200-billion-dollar budget deficit and a 100-billion-dollar trade deficit, and they're interrelated. Are we going to let the Midwest become a wasteland overnight as a matter of national policy? We send Japan low-value soybeans, wheat, corn, coal and cotton. They send us high-value autos, motorcycles, TV sets and oil-well casings. *It's 1776 and we're a colony again, this time of Japan.*

We could, for a change, be tough. The Common Market countries don't get hung up on ideology about free trade. Britain limits Japanese cars to 10 percent of the market. France has a 3 percent lid. Italy: 2,000 Japanese cars a year. They all say: "It's our country and our jobs, and we don't want social problems foisted on us. Our consumers may pay a few bucks more, but otherwise, they'd pay more for unemployment benefits."

Q. Isn't it a bit embarrassing to argue, as you

do, for an extension of Japan's quotas in a year in which auto companies could earn 10 billion dollars in profits? [Note: The Big Three actually earned $9,802,000,000—of which GM accounted for $4,516,000,000; Ford, $2,906,000,000; and Chrysler, $2,380,000,000.]

A. The average American will look at the very big profits of Chrysler this year—not to mention those of GM—and say, "Why don't they reduce prices or stop squawking?" I wish it were that easy.

I've been at Chrysler five years. In that time we've run up $3.5 billion in losses, offset the past nine months by $900 million in profits. I'm still $2.6 billion in the hole. I need breathing room. If you can guarantee me nine more quarters of $350 million dollar profits, then I won't worry much about restraints.

That's what makes horse races. It will be a tough sell to say anybody's hurting when he's making billions. Maybe even Chrysler will make billions—would you have believed that?"

In contrast to Iacocca's style of first-person jabs and counterjabs, often employing such simplistic assertions as "we're a colony again," the same message about Japan's trading edge vis-à-vis the United

States was delivered in gloved-fist style by Iacocca's counterpart at Ford until he retired in January 1985, Philip Caldwell: "If we were on—and I hate to use this phrase all the time, but I can't think of any other one—a level playing field," Caldwell said in a *Fortune* magazine interview published March 4, 1985, "that would be one thing. But we're not, and until we get there, you are forced to take steps you'd rather not.... We could easily get an automative trade deficit with Japan of $27 billion to $28 billion. We're living beyond our means—we aren't able to pay with goods we can sell."

Ever the pragmatist, Iacocca insisted that Chrysler was positioned to survive the boost in Japanese quotas, having slashed its break-even point from 2.4 million cars a year in 1980 to 1.1 million in 1984.

"At the very worst period of a normal cyclical downturn, we will at least break even," he declared. "But long term, I'm not in business to break even. So we would go outside the U.S. to get some of our cars. Right now Chrysler gets only 7 percent of its cars from abroad.

"We're looking at Korea as a possible source. Maybe we'll expand in Mexico. We'll get as efficient, as productive as we can through technology, and we'll attack the $12.50 an hour we pay [per worker] in fringe benefits, including health costs. We may find partners in Europe for joint ventures."

In so ardently battling over a four-year period to rein in the Japanese new-car importers, Iacocca undoubtedly served the purpose of giving Chrysler "breathing room" of its own to stage its unprecedented comeback from the emergency room. At the same time, his sometimes unbridled passion rubbed many power centers and power leaders the wrong way—not least the White House, the Japanese (including Chrysler's Mitsubishi partners), and the senior executives of General Motors, foes of quotas and suppliers of several key components to Chrysler.

Those are the risks of being a contentious company chairman. Iacocca had nothing to lose when Chrysler needed all the help and publicity it could get. But the enemies one makes during a crusade may not be so forgiving in the event of a future Chrysler crunch.

18

"ALL THE THRUST

OF A RACING CAR"

"DON'T KNOCK A CUSTOMER—OR A would-be customer." That has been a cardinal rule of American corporate executives; following it, they maintain the appearance of political neutrality, though the overriding majority have privately sided with Republican candidates except in depression or war years. And that was Lee Iacocca's inclination as president of Ford: apolitical in public statements, mostly liberal Republican in personal preferences.

Iacocca's move to the presidency and chairmanship of Chrysler changed his posture toward public issues almost full circle. Never an admirer of the U.S. political process, which he regards as too slow,

Iacocca for the first time in his life was forced to become an intimate player in that process as a supplicant for federal loan guarantees needed to bail out Chrysler. From that point on, Iacocca decided to speak out on issues he thought relevant to the future both of the resurgent Chrysler and of the nation as a whole, whether would-be customers and the Reagan administration liked it or not.

Whether Iacocca's candor is exemplary for other businessmen on their oratorical rounds is debatable, given the power of governmental authority these days. Iacocca's image as an outspoken, fearless, even adamant advocate was undeniably enhanced—and this rounded out the public concept of him as not only a product huckster but as a public-minded "leader" as well.

Iacocca speaks in "tommy-gun" fashion. He drums out his lines with intensity, not demurring from street jargon or even milder four-letter words to make a point. He uses the first person words "I" and "we" a great deal. He prods opponents of his views by name, up to and including President Reagan or Democrats like Senator William Proxmire.

He is not averse to patriotic or idealistic sentiments. He tells few jokes, being one of industry's few speakers whose drill-sergeant style carries an audience along amazingly well by itself. He is a practiced and effective respondent to audience and media questions—sometimes to the point of redundant excess.

A sampler of Iacocca reflections and responses after a career of thirty-nine years follows, presented here to delineate the verbal style of a top-ranked executive who has been featured on the cover of *Time* magazine no fewer than four times.

On UAW demands at Ford in 1970:

"Who am I to say what we have produced in this country?... I don't now why some guys won't accept discipline. Maybe it's because they're young.... I don't know why they won't recognize established order, like getting to work at eight. The son-of-a-bitch comes in at 8:40. You ask, 'Didn't I tell you to come in at eight?' You say, 'Well, you bastard, I'll discipline you.' He doesn't recognize discipline or he'd have been there at eight in the first place.

"So rules don't work. You say, 'Ah, we'll use that old American thing, incentive. We'll pay him something if he comes in.' But he's not coming in the fifth day, *now*. If we pay him more, he'll come in three days instead of four."

On his aborted proposal to merge Ford and Chrysler:

"No, we couldn't do it now. They wouldn't let us—I don't think the law would allow it. There was only one window, I think, and it passed.

"I mean, Toyota and GM getting together really tests the antitrust laws, but Ford and Chrysler getting together on the basis there would be more competition, not less, might be a tough sell.

"I try to be as objective as I can because I know both companies so well. It would have been fantastic. It would have been as big as GM almost in a fortnight. Bigger than GM in Mexico, bigger in Canada... super!"

On his decision to join Chrysler and on his feelings toward his old employer:

"It was the only game in town when I got fired. That's something I won't forgive the bastard for. I came over here and didn't know how bad it was. There were nights when I didn't think I was going to make it....

"I can look Henry Ford right in the eye and say— I put together a better car company with better products than his.... [The Fords] practiced the divine right of kings. They were a cut above even WASPs. They wouldn't even socialize with you. You could produce money for 'em, but you weren't about to hobnob with 'em.... I knew I had to scratch for what I got. Nobody was gonna say, 'There's a nice Italian boy, I'd like to take care of him.'"

To leaders of the Democratic Party:

"Where's the purity of your ideology? Whatever you say about the Republicans, they are ideologically pure to their cause. You are the Chrysler Corporation of American politics.

"Where the hell do you stand? For your district first and your country second or the other way around? Millions of jobs are pouring out of your country. Right now a lot of you are fighting each other instead of fighting the President. . . .

"I just reported $2.4 billion in profit [for 1984]. I'm laughing all the way to the bank. But inside, I'm crying because I get paid to look out three or four years ahead, and I don't like what I see."

On the future of the auto industry:

"I used to say, 'How can I plan in the car business?' and the guy says, 'What's gas?' 'Put in somewhere between $1 and $3 a gallon.' All right, that's our life blood. How about interest rates, our other life blood? 'Well, put down it'll be somewhere between 10 and 20 percent.'

"I say, gee, you've got to give me something closer than that, guys. You can't plan that. Because if those two swing that much, then you say, 'What's your industry?' They say, 'Somewhere between five and 10 million cars!'

"I say I have four factories and 20,000 people— too many at that rate. And that's what makes it tough."

On the Federal Reserve Board:

"I once suggested, 'How about a Federal Business Board?' The Reserve Board controls our destinies—it's all bankers. There's not a businessman on that Board."

On GM's bigness:
"I wish I were in GM's position. It doesn't have to worry about small cars, because it has 85 percent of the large-and-luxury-car market, where the big profit margins are. GM can cultivate that market at whatever cost for labor and turn Ford and Chrysler into the meat in the sandwich, between GM on one side with large cars and the unrestrained imports with their cost advantage on the other."

On Japan's trade position vis-à-vis the United States:
"I'm no Communist, folks, but it's not Russia that's laying waste to my business and to most of the rest of business in this country—it's Japan. Our friend. While we stack up the missiles in the front yard, all aimed at our enemy, our friend is taking over the backyard."

On being President of the United States:
"I'd be a lousy President. It's not having a short fuse. I don't have that spirit of talking things to death and compromising. I'd get into trouble."

To the League of Women Voters annual convention in Detroit in May 1984:
"This is a city that has literally risen from the

ashes over the past 18 months and we are all proud
of and grateful for, I might add, that fact. We at
Chrysler are particularly proud. We had a brush
with death. *The Wall Street Journal*, along with a
lot of others, even said we should 'die with dignity'—
whatever that meant. Right or wrong, we chose not
to.

"That we made it through the graveyard is due
to the efforts of a lot of ordinary people—our suppliers, our bankers, dealers, employees, cities, states,
and the federal government. But it's due mostly to
the goodwill and support of the American people.
Given the chance and given a choice, they opted to
help save the company—and a lot of jobs, I might
add—by buying what they believed to be pretty
good products, even though the company that built
them might not even be around."

About critics of the proposed federal loan guarantees for Chrysler:

Then-Representative David Stockman, a Republican and the only member of the Michigan
Congressional delegation to vote against the loan
guarantee bill: "He was a former divinity student,
but I guess he was playing hooky the day they
learned about compassion." [Stockman became
President Reagan's budget director.]

The Business Roundtable: "These guys are sup-
posed to be the business elite of this country. But
they're a bunch of hypocrites. Their group was

founded by some steel guys who've spent their lives trying to screw the government. Where were you when loan guarantees were made available for steel companies, shipbuilders and airlines?"

About powerful Representative Henry Reuss, then-chairman of the House Banking Committee: "[He] proposed at one point that Chrysler ought to be building railroad cars. We couldn't afford the facilities we had, but this guy thought we should be getting into a whole new line of vehicles."

About the next generation of American kids and their future:

"I've heard it said that our kids will be the first generation of Americans that will have to settle for less than their parents had. I pray to God our kids don't believe that. But I can see how they might.

"Look at the size of the public debt we're saddling them with. We're paying our way today by mortgaging their futures. Our parents didn't do that to us. And they'd be ashamed of *us* for doing it to *our* kids."

Finally, to an interviewer asking how he became "one of the most admired figures in American business at a time when corporate leaders were not terribly admired":

"People love to root for the underdog. There's an appeal to basic values in that—you've come back from the dead, so to speak, you've persevered. I get all this mail that says: 'I was going to declare bankruptcy. But you didn't—so I decided to stick it out, work a little harder and claw my way back up.'

"I guess people identify with me for getting Chrysler back from the precipice....

"It's been hell getting us this far—no fun at all. Now we've got some fantastic products, and the fun is to see how good you can make them."

Iacocca has not been the first prominent corporate chief executive to practice tell-it-like-it-is dialogue and oratory, but he has been the rarest of communicators in that he has sounded off with a track record and with fervor almost without modern precedent.

An admiring Leo Kelmenson, president of the Chrysler ad agency Kenyon & Eckhardt, calls Iacocca a "profound" leader who is "absolutely dedicated to accomplishing whatever it is he has his mind on. He sets his course and attacks; if you get in his way, he'll run over you like an M-1 tank."

A more objective Gail Sheehy, the writer, finds Iacocca "genetically incapable of moderation... [he has] all the thrust of a racing car."

If being heard is half the battle and being believed is the other half, Iacocca is batting a thousand in terms of his primary goal of rescuing and revitalizing Chrysler.

19

FORD'S CHANGES AI ("AFTER IACOCCA")

EE IACOCCA'S PENCHANT FOR QUARTERLY reviews of staffers' performance records, described by many who have endured the system as "management by fear," has been modified by the men who took charge of Ford after Iacocca's presidency was terminated in 1978.

Although the present chairman, Donald E. Petersen, is an unsentimental administrator with a dislike for costly overlapping and for "redundancy" among vice-presidents and senior staff directors, he is a Stanford University Business School alumnus who believes that a "better way" exists than periodic crackings of the whip by a boss over his underlings on a formal basis.

The distinction between Petersen's approach and that of Iacocca is one of philosophy and personal preference. Petersen, when he was president reporting to Philip Caldwell, the immediate past chairman of Ford, equated the style of management practiced in the Iacocca presidency there as linked to the domestic auto industry's "old rigidities, old assumptions." Just as the innovative Petersen set about overhauling Ford's new-car styling, changing it from the popular "box" look to aerodynamic sloping lines, he ordered a drastic transformation in Ford's management system.

Petersen also was willing to learn from Japanese management techniques. What he learned from the Japanese, he says, "had a lot to do with people. . . . If there was any lesson [from Japan], it was simply that we had to change the way we worked with people." He stresses that "today Ford is changing, and in the process we are writing our own book on management."

Iacocca has made no secret of his conviction that the Caldwell-Petersen regime at Ford could not hold a candle to what would have taken place in Dearborn had he risen to the chairmanship in 1980, when Henry Ford II was set to retire. He firmly believes that Chrysler would not have survived without a wholesale shakeup of personnel, followed by an infusion of the tough-line approach on the survivors carried over from Ford.

That Ford measured up to the challenge of the

early-1980s recession, as well as to the morale shock induced by Iacocca's recruitment of so many key Ford personnel to man Chrysler leadership posts, was due to a large extent to the revised management concepts installed by Petersen, who follows in an MBA track shared by such Ford presidents as Robert McNamara and Arjay Miller.

Striking to the heart of Ford's new code, Petersen advocates that "artificial barriers" between management and labor be removed at all levels. (Iacocca, for his part, met this problem by placing the UAW president, Douglas Fraser, on Chrysler's board of directors—a tactic that worked in a different way.) Petersen sought to extend the rapprochement with labor into the plant levels, sending teams of unionists and foremen to study Japanese techinques "over there" and founding "quality work circles" early on at as many plants as possible.

"What the teams found was this," Petersen recalls. "Artificial barriers between people systematically impede progress in both quality and productivity."

The innovative use of teams has resulted in spawning solutions to problems that had defied answers in the past, says Petersen. These areas include job training, job security, and even employment "satisfaction," says Petersen, who adds that Ford has suffered no strikes in five years and has concluded two far-reaching UAW labor agreements in the same timespan.

"We started with the assumption," Petersen states,

"that all of our people have an important contribution to make in building quality into our products. In our plants throughout the world, our people are bringing their enthusiasm, their intelligence and their pride to a task where, before, they too often were just bringing their backs and muscles. We call it Employee Involvement."

As a concrete example of the Employee Involvement approach at work, Petersen tells how a team of sixty-two unionized hourly workers at Ford's Livonia, Michigan, transmission plant helped in changing plant layout and tool design for the company's new 1986-model intermediate-size cars, the Ford Taurus and Mercury Sable.

The Involvement process has brought suppliers into forward product planning as much as three years in advance of model introduction. The supplier of fiberglass roof liners for the Taurus and Sable, the Johns-Manville Corporation, received an almost unheard-of contract from Ford "for the lifetime of the vehicles," the obvious intent being to assure a continuity of service and, it is hoped, quality, while at the same time providing a degree of security in an often tenuous relationship.

In a direct reference to the type of managerial approach favored by Iacocca in his years at Ford, Petersen boasts of the elimination of "barriers" between people in corporate offices: "We're spending less time beefing up organization charts," he explains, "and more time paring them down. We have 25 percent fewer vice presidents at Ford than we did six years ago, and we are moving away from *top-heavy, top-down dictating styles*." (emphasis added)

That last phrase—"top-heavy, top-down dictating styles"—can be interpreted as a jab at the Iacocca method of running a corporation. Actually, Iacocca has given Chrysler's down-under managers much more leeway in making decisions than had been the case at Ford when he was there.

Nevertheless, Petersen and Iacocca do possess distinct personality differences as corporate chairmen. Iacocca is more of a one-man decider—or mover and shaker. He'll throw out ideas and recommendations for implementation by staff, whereas Petersen will solicit a wide range of suggestions and decide in consultation with senior officers.

"We're pushing lines of decision-making farther down in the organization," Petersen says. "We're eliminating unnecessary paperwork, reports, meetings, committees and rigid controls. All this because we believe that people can operate better without artificial barriers that are built into the classic corporate structure."

To implement this managerial "transformation," Ford is budgeting for a multimillion-dollar employee retraining program from the top to the lowest levels. A course called "Participative Management and Employee Involvement" was given in 1984 for more than a thousand of the highest-ranking Ford executives with the expectation, as Petersen puts it, "that the spirit of teamwork and caring and togetherness permeates our entire organization."

Courses imply an academic-type assault on management problems, befitting Petersen, who recalls fondly his student days at Stanford with distinguished economics professors James Howell and Theodore J. Kreps. Petersen is a member of the high-IQ society Mensa and, though he has assimilated the technical and marketing dimensions of a huge automaking corporation, it would not be difficult to picture him teaching finance or management classes at the Wharton or at the University of Michigan business schools.

The Petersen style, however, is not the Iacocca style, and never will be. Both, together with GM's Roger Smith, are seeking to sharpen their companies' competitive postures against each other and, more urgently, the threats from the Far East and Europe. Iacocca is not the tyrant in this endeavor that his critics sometimes allege, but courses and decentralized authority play second fiddle to decisiveness and motivation. "Despite what the textbooks say," Iacocca asserts, "most important decisions in corporate life are made by individuals, not by committees.

"My policy has always been to be democratic all the way to the point of decision. Then I become the ruthless commander."

Iacocca, noting that Ford has established more

committees even than GM (which introduced the "committee system" of corporate management), believes that committees have their place as forums for the sharing of thoughts and intentions. But he warns that over-reliance on committees could shrink efficiency and result in costly delays in marketing and product development. Or, simply put, "Too many cooks spoil the broth."

The successful minivan pioneered by Chrysler in early 1984, for example, had been conceived by Harold Sperlich even during his Ford years and was dormant until Sperlich was joined at Chrysler by Iacocca. No committee cogitated over the minivan, except as to its final execution, and then the front-wheel-drive platforms already in place at Chrysler gave the minivan a powertrain base that Ford lacked in the mid-1970s.

"Without a Sperlich and Iacocca to be the architects and pushers," a Chrysler staffer says, "somebody else would have beaten us to it. It was not a committee-type vehicle to be fussed over by finance, labor, engineering, you name it."

By way of underscoring the role of strong personal advocates in bringing the Chrysler minivan into being a year ahead of everyone else, GM's delay in catching up to the Dodge Caravan and Plymouth Voyager has been one acknowledged reason for the number-one automaker's revolutionary reorganization of its five major car divisions into two semi-autonomous groups. GM has charged each of the groups—Chevrolet-Pontiac-Canada-Saturn and Buick-Oldsmobile-Cadillac—with the task of speeding up new-model development so that it's not caught again by a competitor's breakthrough.

In Petersen's well-conceived philosophy of management, a "people-centered" structure will percolate with ideas because of "an atmosphere that encourages creativity, openness and balanced risk-taking." In short, give the troops their freedom from top-down orders from the officers, and brace yourself for a wave of "unique, productive ideas."

"We are allowing our managers," the Ford chairman explains, "to act more like entrepreneurs, like the owners of their own businesses—to let them know there are rewards for sensible risk-taking.

"When I say 'risk-taking,' I'm not talking about 'seat-of-the-pants' adventurism. I'm not talking about a Las Vegas roll of the dice.

"I'm talking about a reasoned judgment that allows decisions to be made in a timely way—judgment that doesn't require every issue to be studied to the point of total exhaustion. Because when you worry an issue to death, you've closed your options—you've already made a decision to delay. It's easy to say 'no.' But winners in the risk-taking business are those who know when to say 'yes.'

"The tone, then—the atmosphere we set—determines whether the ideas we need will come to light. We are providing what we believe is the right atmosphere for generating creative ideas."

To Iacocca, the essential functions of a manager are twofold: to decide and to motivate. The Petersen theory that "atmosphere" stimulates—almost like the process of biological growth—is too bland for Iacocca, who likes his managers to inspire through direct communication, man-to-man, woman-to-woman, not unlike a salesperson with a customer or client.

The "pitch" is the crux of the Iacocca manager-to-managee formula. A boss should ask his underling to carry out a task. ("Don't leave without asking for the order," he writes.) He believes that managers who fail to listen are asking for disloyalty, and those who never praise an employee's good ideas are inviting hostility.

"You have to be able to listen well if you're going to motivate the people who work for you," contends Iacocca, seeming to agree in part with the nonauthoritarians of the Petersen school. "Right there, that's the difference between a mediocre company and a great company.

"The most fulfilling thing for me as a manager is to watch someone the system has labeled as just average or mediocre really come into his own, all because someone has listened to his problems and helped him solve them."

Where Iacocca differs from Petersen is in the *degree* of how much a manager should assert himself—but that degree could be considerable. Petersen as Ford president turned his stylists loose in concocting a radically different "aerodynamic" concept to replace the boxiness of American cars through the 1970s. The cars from Ford that innovated this styling—the Thunderbird and Tempo families—finally won consumer acceptance after a slow start, but an Iacocca might have "listened" and "helped . . . solve" by ordering less risky designs.

The Petersen approach, as Iacocca learned painfully himself at Ford, does not excuse the top executive from responsibility for the choices of the group. Let the chicks roam, but make sure they're going where you want them to go.

20

A TOUGH ACT

TO FOLLOW?

NOTHING IS FOREVER, NOT EVEN 1985'S COR-
porate superhero. Nor can a top boss as
dominating and flamboyant as Lee Iacocca
hope to find or create an exact clone as a
successor. It's easier at companies with an orderly
pattern of succession for the next commander-in-
chief to turn out as a carbon-copy—or a reasonable
facsimile.

Which brings up the matter of Chrysler's next
command team, and what Iacocca has done or not
done to assure both continuity in management and
financial profit-making. Grave concerns have arisen
about the post-Iacocca Chrysler, stemming from
Iacocca's decision to surround himself in the office

of the chairman with only former Ford associates tuned in to his wavelength: Vice-Chairman Gerald Greenwald, fifty, the finance expert; President Harold Sperlich, fifty-five, Chrysler's product and manufacturing overlord; and the newest recruit, Executive Vice-President Ben Bidwell, fifty-eight, the sales and marketing whiz.

Asked about the efficacy of such a troika-plus-one for steering Chrysler on a continuing growth course if the situation suddenly changes to a troika-minus-one, Bidwell replies: "I know what you're thinking. Here's this drum major high-stepping down the street. Is there a band behind him? Or is the band four blocks back or even on the same block? I understand that. Would everybody fall on their ass?"

Answering his own question, Bidwell assures the interviewer that the triad below the chairman "get along pretty well, have a reasonably good sense of our turf and strike a pretty good balance."

For their parts, Greenwald is looking at a five-year "rolling" product spending program of about $10.5 billion, and Sperlich is finalizing—for yet another phase in Chrysler's checkered history—cars challenging GM's hold on the upscale sedan and coupe market. Have no fear, chorus the Iacocca threesome. There is "life" for Chrysler after he's gone.

Yet such evaluators as *Automotive News* see troubles ahead. "Regardless of his departure date, to consider Chrysler without Iacocca is to view the auto company as a business entity with strengths and weaknesses apart from the Iacocca personality," reporter Dan McCosh wrote in the issue of March 25, 1985.

"Such exercise reveals a company more complex than the swashbuckling one-man show often portrayed, a company still scrambling for a definitive niche in a rapidly internationalizing auto industry."

An informed Ford insider says that Henry Ford II believed that Iacocca as chief executive officer of Ford would have been so flamboyant and monarchial that the company would have been left rudderless when the time came for Iacocca to step aside.

By contrast, the early 1985 transition at Ford from the chairmanship of Philip Caldwell to that of Donald Petersen was the smoothest change at the top in Ford history. It resembled the GM formula since the chaos of the William C. Durant years in the early 1920s—a system installed by Alfred P. Sloan, Jr., and copied by droves of U.S. corporations ever since.

Iacocca, however, is so indelibly linked to Chrysler and its products that even members of the "troika" around him shudder to think of the fallout if he were compelled to bow out early. "There's an awareness gap that has to be closed," admits a key Chrysler marketing official, "but it's harder than the devil to divorce Iacocca from the products. He knows it, too, but not much has been done about it."

By the same token, Iacocca's insistence on loyalty and his eviction of nearly all former Chrysler vice-presidents run the risk of leaving his heirs apparent and the retinue of vice-presidents without the innovative creativity needed to meet the changing marketplaces later on. The staff may have become too reliant on Iacocca, much as Colbert foundered when he took charge of Chrysler after Keller and as Riccardo stumbled after Townsend.

"An excellent chairman may be a Snow White," says Robert H. Rock, a Philadelphia management consultant, commenting on companies managed by dynamos like Iacocca. "But if the course is misguided, seven dwarfs won't present the diversity of opinions and experiences that will formulate alternative directions."

Lacking such diversity of input with Iacocca still running the show, what can be expected when Iacocca has moved away to his rendezvous with whatever? If he awakens to this problem, the most likely course would call for him to stay on as chairman but cede the chief executive officer's role to one of the other three men in the office of the chairman.

To Iacocca, that would constitute abdication. Besides, a grateful board of directors has offered him bountiful stock options if he remains as the chief (although what's been done can be undone as need be by the usually subservient board). Iacocca's appetite to be king could ironically thus stand in the way of Chrysler's future.

There are those who dismiss the razzmatazz surrounding Iacocca and find him a less than exemplary corporate manager, ruling by intimidation rather than professional expertise. But in a sense, every business chief carries with his decision-making authority an element of "rule by fear" of being fired, demoted, or bypassed. Iacocca, by the sheer force of his personality, appears to be more of a bully than most of his counterparts at other corporations. The fact is that he combines his character strength with a knowledgeability and grasp that are awesome in a top executive facing so many disparate decisions to make or to unmake. A "mouth" alone would not have saved Chrysler.

As Chrysler began preparations to launch its 1986 models, Iacocca appeared to be giving the thought of retirement or of an altogether new career backburner consideration at best. In a typical show of business pragmatism, he announced a deal with Chrysler's Mitsubishi partner to build a new plant in the United States for small-car assembly late in the 1980s. This after years of Iacocca's scorching the Japanese trade imbalance with the United States and publicly embarrassing the Mitsubishi management.

At the same time, the indefatigable Iacocca went on to Korea to cement an auto parts manufacturing arrangement with a South Korean firm. A car manufacturing compact with the South Koreans, whose labor rates are only about two to three dollars an hour, lies ahead for Chrysler.

As *Time* magazine said of him in its fourth cover story on Iacocca on April 1, 1985, "Iacocca likes it best when he can make managing a car company seem like a martial task, urgent and vast and possibly heroic."

Nevertheless, the big tour and the press announcements staged like movie scenes are not the essential ingredients of the Iacocca mystique as a corporate manager. In a sense, while the pizzazz has boosted his stock personally and indisputably rubbed off on Chrysler's product appeal, he could not have achieved the exalted status of "super-leader" in American industry without basic notions of mission and execution. Past Chrysler top executives had lost sight of these fundamentals as the world around them changed. Iacocca learned many of these skills at Ford and then applied them at Chrysler.

When Iacocca arrived in 1978, Chrysler was a stricken company; the situation forced the institution of drastic life-saving measures foreign to his Ford experience. Not least of these—indeed the most challenging and most critical to Chrysler's ultimate survivability—were the upgrading of product quality and the overhaul of a complacent management team equated with unacceptable quality.

That this led to a more efficiently run organization, lacking the layers of authority that had characterized Chrysler in the past, was a welcome by-product as far as Iacocca is concerned. The astounding 1984 fiscal results, so spectacularly reversed from the waves of red ink in the late 1970s and early 1980s, are a testament to Iacocca's success in slashing the break-even point across the board and then keeping sales at high levels during a strong new-car and truck market—a double-edged windfall that had eluded Chrysler in the past.

Can Chrysler "cope" without its Indiana Jones? There are those who say no, that the organization was and is energized by him and will lose its vitality and even *raison d' être* in his wake. Others believe he has performed so ably as a rebuilder that the edifice will remain sturdy under one or another of his handpicked flag officers.

As for Iacocca himself, as he exercises during a typical ten-hour day in the gym he had built on Chrysler's executive office floor, he relishes the almost daily media coverage of his activities and the descriptions of him as one of the first, if not the first, widely admired and almost beloved American heroes out of the business world. John D. Rockefeller, Andrew Carnegie, even Henry Ford II drew respect, even fear, but never applause from their workers or requests for autographs, photographs, and addresses in the thousands every week.

"Heroes are created by popular demand, sometimes out of the scantiest materials," wrote Gerald

White Johnson in his 1943 book *American Heroes and Hero Worship*, "...such as the apple that William Tell never shot, the ride that Paul Revere never finished, the flag that Barbara Fritchie never waved."

In Lee Iacocca's case, style and substance sprang from solid materials, waiting to be applied at the right moment. The right moment came along, and a manager-hero emerged.

ABOUT THE AUTHOR

MAYNARD M. GORDON WAS AN AUTO INDUSTRY "watcher" even before Lee Iacocca started his career at Ford. Gordon's journalistic career began forty-one years ago when as a student at Detroit's Wayne State University, he joined the staff of *Automotive News*, the industry's trade weekly. After a stint in the Army, he returned to *Automotive News* as news editor until 1962, when he bought the weekly newsletter *Motor News Analysis*. He has been its publisher and editor ever since.